The Horse Illustrated Guide to

English Riding

BY LESLEY WARD

The Horse Illustrated Guide to

English Riding

BY LESLEY WARD

BOWTIE™
P R E S S

A Division of Fancy Publications
Irvine, California

Ruth Berman, editor-in-chief
Nick Clemente, special consultant
Cover and book design copyright © 1998 by Michele Lanci-Altomare

The horses in this book are referred to as *he* or *she* in alternating chapters unless their gender is apparent from the activity discussed.

The photograph on page 82 is courtesy of © Bob Langrish.

Library of Congress Cataloging-in-Publication Data

Ward, Lesley.
  The horse illustrated guide to English riding / Lesley Ward.
      p.   cm.
    ISBN 1-889540-11-0 (alk. paper)
    1. Horsemanship.   2. Horsemanship- -Pictorial works.   I. Title.
  SF309. W268   1998
  798.2- -dc 21   98-20542
                                                            CIP

BowTie™ Press
3 Burroughs
Irvine, California 92618

Manufactured in the United States of America
First Printing September 1998
10 9 8 7 6 5 4 3 2 1

ACKNOWLEDGMENTS

I would like to thank the following people
for their help with this book:

Pat Bailey of the Club, San Juan Capistrano, CA; Sharon Biggs;

Lynn Elliott; Liz Erickson; Jane Frusher; Stacey Hall; Moira Harris;

Ashley Kohler; Katie McKay; Lindsay Mickelson; Dylan Lake;

Laura Loda; Julie Mignery; Barbara Provence; Marissa Uchimura;

and finally my father, Alan Ward, for his excellent editing skills.

CONTENTS

Learning to ride English style is a challenging goal, but once you master the basic skills, it won't be long before you're cantering on trails, clearing fences, and learning fancy dressage movements.

Riding keeps you fit, makes you feel good, and is a lot of fun! Soon you'll be hooked, and horses will become a major part of your life. One lesson a week will turn into three. You'll start helping out at the barn. You'll trade in your jeans for breeches. Soon, the sales assistant at the local tack shop will know you by name. Eventually, you'll start scanning the Classified Ads for horses for sale. There's no escape from the world of horses.

But let's be realistic. First you have to take regular lessons and spend hours in the saddle. Becoming a good rider doesn't happen overnight. Most of us work really hard and ride a lot of horses before we become experienced riders.

It's essential that you find a friendly, patient instructor. Even Olympic riders have coaches. Why? Because even such experienced riders know that no matter how confident you become about your riding ability or how naturally talented you are, you never stop learning. Every time you mount a new horse, jump around a strange course, or take a fall, you add to your knowledge of horses and riding.

This book tells you how to develop an excellent riding position and a secure seat so that you can communicate effectively with a horse. It also teaches you how to ride a horse at any speed and over fences. Read this book before you head for your riding lessons, and use it over and over as a reference. So what are you waiting for? Happy reading and riding!

*Once you master the basic
skills of horsemanship,
the sky's the limit!*

GETTING STARTED

IF YOU WANT TO IMPROVE YOUR RIDING SKILLS, the most important thing you should do is find a good riding instructor and sign up for lessons. If you don't have your own horse, you can take lessons at a riding school or with an instructor who has his or her own string of school horses. If you are lucky enough to have your own horse—but are new to riding—it might be a good idea to board your horse at a barn that has an experienced instructor.

CHOOSING A RIDING SCHOOL

Check the bulletin board at your local tack shop for signs advertising local riding schools or instructors. Ask the sales assistant if she can recommend any decent schools or reputable instructors.

Also, look in the *Yellow Pages* of your telephone book for any riding schools near you. There may be several advertised, but it's impossible to tell from an ad if the school is good. If you have a friend who already rides there, ask her opinion. If she likes it, call the manager and ask to look around during lessons.

When you arrive, stop by the office and see the manager. She may want to give you a quick tour around the barn, or she may send you

Take lessons from a qualified instructor.

The barn area should be neat and tidy.

off by yourself to have a snoop. When walking around, keep the following in mind:

The Staff: The riding-school employees should be friendly and dressed in appropriate clothing for riding—such as jodhpurs or jeans and boots, not shorts and sandals. No one should be smoking around the barn area. Safety-minded horse folk know that one spark can ignite a bale of hay and cause a fire. Barn workers should be kind but firm with the horses. You shouldn't see anyone shouting at or beating horses.

The Barn: The stable area at a responsible riding school is tidy. Manure and used bedding is swept neatly on a muck heap, away from the barn. You won't see litter on the ground. Peek over a couple of stable doors and check the cleanliness. If horses are standing in piles of manure or puddles of urine, it's best to leave and find another school.

The buildings should be in good repair. You should not spot broken glass or equipment with sharp edges that could hurt you or a horse. Stroll out to the fields or turn-out areas. No rusty farm equipment or garbage should clutter these areas.

The horses should look healthy and happy.

The Horses and Ponies: Check that the school's horses and ponies look alert and interested in what is going on around them. They must be well groomed and have shiny, healthy-looking coats. You can be less critical in winter when it's hard to keep horses and ponies completely mud-free, especially if they spend time in a field.

The horses must look well fed—you shouldn't be able to see their ribs. Don't ride at a school where the horses look tired and in poor condition. Ask how many times a day a horse is ridden. He should be used for no more than three lessons a day. Don't hand over your money to ride a horse who has been ridden more than that.

The Lessons: Watch a lesson or two. Does the school match students and horses by size and ability? If you're petite, you don't want to get stuck riding a giant horse because your legs may not be effective on his sides. Plus, you may not be strong enough to control him. And if you're just learning to ride you don't want to be assigned a frisky horse. Do the lesson horses seem well behaved and fairly obedient?

School horses can be sluggish, and sometimes they ignore their rider's aids. This is fairly normal. Who can blame them? Being ridden by bouncy beginners every day is no picnic! But if the riders seem to be having serious problems with their horses, this may not be a reputable school. There should be no bucking, kicking, rearing, or bolting in a class for novice riders.

The horses should be wearing simple, well-fitting tack. It doesn't have to be brand-new, but it should be clean and in good condition. Ideally, the horses should be wearing snaffle bits, but stronger horses may have Kimberwickes or Pelhams in their mouths. Avoid a barn that uses gag bits or hackamores because they are severe and should be used by experienced riders only.

Do the students wear safety helmets? Even the safest, quietest horse can spook or stumble, causing his rider to fall. A truly responsible, safety-conscious instructor insists that her students wear approved helmets. The instructor should also wear a helmet when mounted to set a good example for her students.

And finally, are all the students in a class of the same riding level and approximate age group? If you're a beginner, you don't want to be stuck in a class with riders jumping 3-foot fences. You want to be with people at your level. For adults, it can be frustrating to ride in a class with an eight-year-old whiz kid who is already jumping courses!

CHOOSING A RIDING INSTRUCTOR

Do some investigating before signing up with an instructor. Why? Because in the United States there is no licensing system. Anyone can put up a sign stating that he or she is an instructor, and many of these people are not qualified to teach. Ask your friends if they can recommend an experienced instructor with a good reputation.

If someone sounds good, call her and let her know how much riding you have done and what sort of riding activities you would like to do. You should enjoy chatting with the instructor. She should be pleasant and sound knowledgeable. Ask how long she has been teaching and about her riding experiences. A good instructor has ridden and competed successfully for many years.

Try to find an instructor who has been through the American Riding Instructor Certification Program. The American Riding Instructors Association (ARIA) tests instructors to make sure they are qualified to teach riding. You can write to the ARIA for a list of certified instructors in your area (see the appendix for the address). These instructors should be professional and safety conscious, as well as insured—another important thing you must check for when looking for an instructor.

When browsing through the ads in your local horse magazine, you'll notice that many instructors specialize in one equestrian sport, for example, dressage, eventing, or show jumping. If you're just starting your riding career, you don't really require a specialist. You want a good, all-around instructor who can teach you the basics of riding in a safe, fun manner. Then, when you are ready, you can decide if one particular equestrian sport is for you. If you're really keen to learn dressage, however, by all means call up a dressage instructor.

Ask what the instructor charges, and then ask your friends how much they pay to get an idea of the going rate. Some instructors give a discount if you pay for a large number of lessons up front. Individual lessons cost more than group ones.

A good instructor gives you plenty of attention.

Once you've found an instructor you like, ask if you can drop by and watch her teach. She shouldn't mind. Here are some signs of a good instructor:

She is patient and doesn't mind explaining things.

Her classes are small and each student gets plenty of attention.

Her horses are well mannered and can do what is asked of them.

Her students look confident and appear to be having a good time.

Her classes are varied and students do not spend the entire lesson working on the same thing.

She doesn't shout at or bully her students.

If you like what you see, book some lessons. The instructor will give you a release form to sign before she lets you on one of her horses.

This form usually states that you understand riding is a dangerous sport and you will not hold the instructor responsible if you get hurt.

The first few lessons you take may be private. This is so the instructor can determine how well you ride and place you in a class that suits your needs.

WHAT YOU SHOULD WEAR TO RIDE

It's not necessary to buy expensive riding clothes right away. A pair of well-fitting jeans and boots or low-heeled shoes with laces are fine for your first two or three lessons. Never wear sneakers because you need heels to keep your feet in the stirrups.

After a couple of lessons, you should know if you're going to continue riding. If you are, it's time to pay a visit to the local tack shop. Here's the basic gear you need if you plan to ride regularly.

A riding helmet: A helmet is your most important item of safety gear. Never ride without one. Buy an ASTM/SEI-approved safety-riding helmet that meets the tough standards set by the American Society for Testing and Materials and has the Safety Equipment Institute seal. Buy one at a tack shop and have it properly fitted. Try on several brands to find one that fits you. Using your hands, wiggle each helmet you try on. The right size fits snugly and does not move at all. Don't try to save money by buying a used helmet because you may not be able to tell just by looking at it if it has been dented or damaged.

There are several types of helmets. Velvet hats with peaks are used in the show ring because they look elegant. Jockey skullcaps are used by jockeys and eventers (people who jump cross-country). Most riders cover a skullcap with a hat cover. Schooling helmets look like lightweight bicycle helmets. They have vents to keep your head cool. Make sure any helmet you buy has a permanent chin strap so it stays on your head if you take a tumble.

Invest in a safety helmet with a chin strap.

Dress appropriately from head to toe.

Footwear: Your riding footwear should have low heels, otherwise your feet slip out of the stirrups, which is dangerous. If you're new to riding, you could invest in a pair of inexpensive, tall, rubber boots. They look pretty good, and you can rinse them off with a hose when they get dirty.

If you can afford it, leather boots are a good investment. Looked after properly, they last for years. Buy them slightly tight around your lower leg as they stretch out fairly quickly. There are two main types of tall boot: dress boots, which are plain; and field boots, which have laces in the front. Dress boots are usually used by people who do dressage. You can also wear short paddock boots. They are ankle high and have laces.

Breeches: Jeans or trousers are acceptable for riding lessons, but as soon as you can afford them, buy a pair of breeches or jodhpurs. Because they are stretchy, they're more comfortable and won't rub your legs like jeans do. Jodhpurs go down to your feet and are worn with short boots. Breeches are shorter and are worn with tall boots.

Jodhpurs and breeches come in many colors. As a beginner, buy them in beige so you can wear them in shows. White breeches are often used by dressage riders and show jumpers in competitions.

When you try on breeches or jodhpurs at the tack store, take a look at yourself in the four-way mirror. Breeches and jodhpurs are not always the most flattering clothing. Make sure they are snug, but not too tight.

Chaps: Chaps are leather leggings that are usually worn over jeans for casual riding only. They aren't permitted in an English-style show. Chaps are great for winter riding because they help keep your legs warm. They fasten with side zippers and are used to protect your clothes. They also help prevent your legs from chafing, but they must fit snugly or they'll rub your legs and make them sore. Buy them slightly tight, as they stretch. Some people have themselves measured and order custom-made chaps, which are very nice.

Half chaps are usually worn with breeches. They cover your lower leg and fasten with zippers or Velcro. Many riders wear them instead of tall boots because they are quick and easy to put on and they give you a good grip on your horse's sides.

Gloves: Gloves are essential because they protect your hands from blisters and give you a firm grip on the reins in wet weather. Leather gloves are nice, but cloth gloves with rubber grips are less expensive and do a good job.

GAINING EXPERIENCE

Once you've begun lessons and have the correct riding gear, you might find that you want to spend more time around horses. Here are some ways to gain valuable experience and have fun too!

Chaps are for casual riding.

Offer to groom and tack up your lesson horse: Arrive a half hour early for your lesson and offer to get your lesson horse ready. This is a great chance for you to get to know the horse, plus you'll learn how to groom and tack up. Afterward, ask if you can untack your horse and feed him.

Volunteer for the North American Riding for the Handicapped Association (NARHA): There are many riding programs for people with disabilities. These programs always need volunteers. You might be called upon to groom and tack up horses. You may lead horses around the ring, or you could be a "sidewalker"—someone who helps the riders keep balanced. Write to NARHA to find a program in your area.

Exercise other people's horses: Many people are too busy to ride their horses enough and are willing to let other people exercise them. Your instructor might know of people who need this help.

NARHA puts horsey volunteers to work.

Offer to exercise other people's horses for them.

Be a horse-show volunteer: Most shows need volunteers to do things such as open gates, help judges, and move fences around. Volunteering is a great way to learn about shows, study riders in action, meet local horse folk, and make new friends. Combined training events rely on volunteers to keep their shows running smoothly. Write to your local dressage, show jumping, or combined training organizations and offer your help.

Be a Pony Club or 4-H volunteer or leader: These equestrian youth clubs desperately need adults to help at rallies, meetings, and shows. Write or call the local Pony Club District Commissioner or your county's agricultural extension office and offer your services.

Attend clinics: Many facilities offer clinics given by top riders and trainers. Even if you don't have a horse, you can usually pay a small fee and attend as a spectator. You will learn a lot about riding and horsemanship by simply watching and listening.

Go on a riding vacation: Browse through horse magazines to find travel companies that offer riding holidays in far-off places. You could go hunting in Ireland, study dressage in Britain, or trail ride through the French countryside. You could also chase steers on a dude ranch in Wyoming or ride a mule in the Grand Canyon. There are plenty of exciting holidays on offer, so start requesting brochures now!

Offer to be a horse-sitter: Post a sign at the barn or tack store advertising yourself as a horse-sitter. People going away on vacation might ask you to groom, feed, and turn out their horses. Maybe you'll get to ride too.

IN THE SADDLE

WHEN YOU START RIDING, IT IS IMPORTANT TO start with the basics. It may be great fun to saddle a horse and gallop down a trail right away, but you won't be learning the skills that make you a good rider. In fact, you may pick up bad habits that will be difficult to get rid of later. So start with a qualified instructor who can teach you correct riding positions the first time you mount a horse. You must learn how to walk and trot safely and properly before you canter, gallop, and jump.

FIT TO RIDE

It helps to be fit and flexible to ride. You'll never improve if you huff and puff after thirty seconds of sitting trot. Regular exercise and staying in shape will make you a better rider, and you'll look better in a pair of breeches! Stay in shape by swimming or riding a bike. Join an aerobics class. You can burn up calories and improve your muscles around the barn, too. Mucking out a stable or lugging bales of hay is terrific exercise, and you can do these chores without hiring an expensive personal trainer!

LEADING A HORSE

Before you mount your horse, learn how to lead her. While standing on your horse's left side and facing forward, lift both reins over her head and

When leading a horse, hold the reins with both hands.

hold on to them with your right hand, about 3 inches below her chin. Hold the excess reins with your left hand. Don't let the reins drag on the ground because your horse could step on them and break them.

Stand next to the horse's shoulder, and when you walk forward, she should walk on too. Some horses obey voice commands, so you may have to say "walk on" when you want your horse to move. When you want her to stop, give a small tug on the reins with your right hand, say "whoa," and stop. If your horse doesn't halt, give one or two gentle tugs on the reins. If she still won't come to a stop, bend your right arm, stick your elbow in front of her chest to form a barrier, and lean into her. Jab her several times with your arm and say "whoa" again. Try not to let your horse bully you when you're leading her because she'll soon realize that she's stronger and will barrel right over you.

MOUNTING A HORSE

It's essential that you mount your horse as gently and quickly as you can, causing her as little stress and strain on her back as possible. If you're athletic and agile, it should be easy to mount your horse. Three bounces on your right foot and you should spring into the saddle—no problem.

But there are bad ways to mount a horse, too. Grabbing the saddle and heaving yourself up onto your horse can twist the saddletree and damage your expensive saddle. And pulling yourself up inch by inch is also wrong. It puts unnecessary strain on your horse's delicate back. It's no wonder many horses fidget and move away when they are about to be mounted.

There are ways to mount that do not damage the saddle or injure your horse, and if you are fit and flexible you should master them quickly.

From the Ground

1. Test that your stirrups are the right lengths. An easy way to tell is to run your stirrups down, face your horse's side, stretch out your right arm straight in front of you, and

Test the stirrup length before you mount.

touch the saddle with your knuckles. Lift the stirrup iron with your left hand and pull it toward you under your right arm. The iron should hit your right armpit. If it doesn't, lengthen or shorten the stirrup leather as appropriate. This is just an approximate measurement; you may still have some adjustments to make when you mount.

2. Make sure the girth is snug. If it's loose, the saddle will move when you mount, and it could end up under your horse's stomach.

3. Stand at your horse's left shoulder and face her tail.

4. Hold the reins with your left hand and the stirrup iron with your right. Slip your left foot into the stirrup. If you can't reach the stirrup, it may be necessary to let it down a few holes until you get your foot into it.

5. Grab some mane with your left hand (the one holding the reins) or rest it on your horse's neck. Place (don't grab) your right hand on the

Stand facing your horse's hindquarters and put your left foot in the stirrup.

Bounce around until you face your horse.

Bounce once or twice and jump up.

Swing your right leg over and sit down gently.

saddle's pommel or seat. Then bounce around on your right foot until you are facing your horse's head. Try not to kick her in the ribs. Give three big bounces and hop lightly into the air.

6. Slowly raise your right leg over your horse's back. Do it in one continuous motion. (This is why you have to be fit!) Try not to bang your leg on the horse's hindquarters.

7. Gently lower yourself into the saddle. Never slam down on a horse's back—this hurts her. Next, put your right foot in the right stirrup.

8. Finally, make sure your stirrup leathers are lying flat against the saddle. If they're twisted, you need to adjust them so they don't rub you.

From a Mounting Block

Sometimes you may need help when mounting a horse. She could be too big for you to get on by yourself, or she may have an extrasensitive back and must be mounted gently. This is when a mounting block comes in handy. A stable or riding school will generally have one.

Walk the horse so her left side is next to the block, ask her to halt, then climb aboard.

A Leg Up

A friend can help you mount by giving you a leg up. Here's how it's done:

1. Stand facing the horse and lift up your left leg. Your friend stands behind you and grabs your lower left leg, below the knee, with both hands.

Using a mounting block puts less stress on a horse's back.

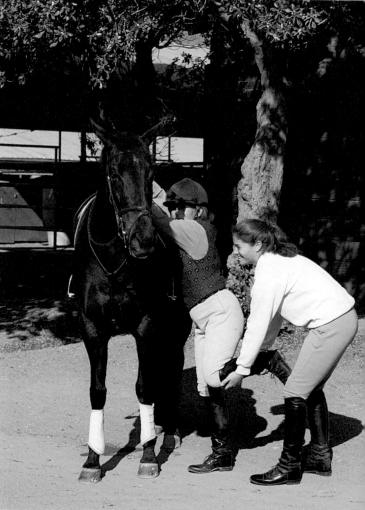

A friend can give you a leg up.

2. Bounce three times, counting with your friend, and on the third bounce, leap up while your friend lifts you in the air. (Be careful that your friend doesn't toss you too high because you might fly over the horse and land on the ground. Practice getting a leg up on a quiet horse.)

3. Swing your right leg over the horse's back and lower yourself into the saddle.

ONCE YOU ARE MOUNTED
Check the Girth

Once you are mounted, check the girth again. Some wily horses suck air into their stomachs when you tighten the girth the first time. Then they let the air out after you mount, leaving the girth loose, allowing the saddle to slip.

Hold your left leg up and lift the saddle flap to check if the girth needs to go up a hole or two.

After three bounces, jump up while your pal lifts you into the saddle.

You can tighten your girth while in the saddle.

Adjust Your Stirrups

Before you set off, make sure your stirrups are the correct lengths. Take both feet out of the stirrups and hang your legs down. Your ankles should hit the bottom of the stirrups. If the stirrups are too long or too short, you can adjust them without dismounting. Place your foot back in the stirrup and lift your leg up and away from the saddle so your weight is not on the stirrups or leathers. Then, lift the saddle skirt up so you can reach the buckle easily. Shorten or lengthen the stirrup leathers as needed.

Dismounting

It's a lot easier to get off a horse than on. Just follow these steps:

1. Take both feet out of the stirrups. Hold both reins in your left hand. Rest your right hand on the saddle or your horse's withers.

2. Gently swing your right leg over your horse's back, face to the right, and slide off.

3. Put both your legs together and bend at the knees as you drop toward the ground. Bending helps soften your landing.

When dismounting, take both feet out of the stirrups.

Swing your right leg over your horse's hindquarters.

Keep your legs together and slide down.

Bend your legs when you land on the ground.

An example of a good position

PERFECTING
YOUR POSITION

Once you've mounted, it's time to work on your position—the way you sit in the saddle. It's very important to develop a good riding position from day one. You'll never improve as a rider if you don't have a decent riding position.

Your goal is to have a "secure seat," which means you stick close to the saddle and don't bounce around. You want to move *with* your horse so you don't interfere with her natural movement. The way you sit on your horse's back influences the way she moves. If you lean one way, she may lean that way too. If you fall forward on her neck, you may unbalance her and cause her to stumble. If you lean back, you might lose control. But if you sit quietly in the saddle and stay in sync with your horse's movements, you'll get the best performance out of her.

Make a point of watching many different riders. The successful ones have the ability to sit quietly on a horse and look as if they are not doing much. It may take awhile before you feel that you're moving with your horse instead of bumping around, but don't worry. If you spend enough time in the saddle, maintaining a good position comes naturally.

Here's an example of a good riding position starting at the top of the body and working our way down. This is the position you should strive for every time you hop into the saddle:

Head: Hold your head up and look between your horse's ears. Always look in the direction you're going. Tipping your head down affects your balance and influences the way your horse moves.

Shoulders: Don't hunch up. Push your shoulders back and down. Try to relax.

Chest: Keep your upper body straight. Stick out your chest slightly. Imagine there's a string attached to the top of your head, pulling you upward.

Back: Your back should be slightly arched, but not stiff. Let it be flexible and move with your horse.

Seat and Thighs: Sit squarely in the middle of the saddle, on the lowest part of the seat. Your seat bones (not your whole rear end) should be as close to the saddle as possible. Sit on both seat bones and distribute your weight as evenly as you can. Hang your legs down naturally and keep your thighs close to the saddle.

Arms: Keep your upper arms glued to your sides. Your elbows should be close to your body, too. If your arms are in the correct position, you should be able to imagine a straight line from your elbows to your hands all the way through the reins to the bit.

Distribute your weight evenly on both seat bones.

Keep your palms facing each other and your thumbs on top.

Hands: When you ride, you use the reins to steer and stop your horse. How a horse performs has a lot to do with how you hold the reins. Your hands should be level with each other, knuckles facing outward, palms facing each other an inch or two apart.

Grip the reins with the middle three fingers of each hand. Keep these fingers firmly closed to keep the reins from slipping out of your hands. Rest your thumbs on top of the reins. Your pinkie fingers go under the reins to keep them in place.

Legs: Your knees can touch the saddle, but don't grip tightly with them. Squeezing with your knees can tip your upper body forward. Your lower legs should be close to your horse's sides, slightly behind the girth. Looking down, you should see only the tips of your toes.

Feet: The balls of your feet should rest on the stirrups with your toes slightly higher than your heels. If your toes point down, your lower leg is thrown out of position, making it difficult to keep your balance. Your feet should be even on both sides of your horse.

Your stirrups must be even on both sides.

Doing exercises, such as airplanes, can limber you up.

EXERCISES AND STRETCHES

Doing exercises and stretches in the saddle is a good way to work on your position. They help you relax and feel comfortable in the saddle. They also limber you up and improve your balance. You can do most exercises at the halt or the walk—you may find them easier to do while your teacher lunges you on a long line. If you do them by yourself, tie your reins in a knot so you can steer easily with one hand. Make sure you exercise on a calm, obedient horse.

Forward Stretches: Hold the reins in one hand, then lean forward and touch your horse's ears with the other hand. Switch the reins to the other hand and repeat the stretch with the opposite hand. Try to keep your lower legs in good riding position near the girth. If you're feeling brave and you're on a lunge line, try reaching back to touch your horse's tail.

Airplanes: Hold the reins with one hand and stretch your other arm out horizontally. Make four or five big circles with your arm, then switch hands and repeat with the other arm. If you're on the lunge, circle both arms at the same time.

Stretch down to do toe touches.

Toe Touches: Hold the reins in your left hand and with your right hand reach over the horse's neck and touch your left toe. Repeat with the other hand and opposite leg.

Ankle Twists: Take both feet out of the stirrups and makes circles in the air with them to loosen your ankle muscles.

Leg lifts really strengthen your thigh muscles.

Leg Lifts: Take both feet out of the stirrups and slowly lift your legs up and as far away from the saddle as you can. Hold them up for a couple of seconds, then lower them slowly back into position at your horse's sides.

The Walk

When learning to ride, you must start at the walk—the slowest, easiest gait to control. Once you can manage your horse at a slow speed, move on to more exciting, speedy activities.

THE AIDS

Before you begin the walk, you must learn the signals that tell a horse what you want him to do. These are called aids, and they help you control and communicate with your horse. There are natural aids and artificial aids.

A horse understands the aids that were taught to him when he was young, usually by his first rider or trainer. You may get on a new horse and ask him to move using the aids you have learned, but he may not understand what you want him to do. It sometimes takes awhile to get used to a new horse.

Aids are signals you give your horse that tell him what to do.

Carry a whip so it rests on your thigh.

Natural Aids

Natural aids come from you: your legs, hands, seat, and voice.

Legs: Squeezing your horse with your lower legs tells him to move forward, sideways, or backward.

Hands: Your hands hold the reins, which attach to the bit. Use your hands to turn a horse or slow him down.

Seat: How you sit affects your horse's movement. When you sit deep in the saddle, he may slow down. Leaning forward tells him to go faster. Shifting your weight to one side or the other may tell him to turn.

Voice: Some horses are trained to obey voice commands. For example, if you cluck to a horse, he may go faster. If you say "whoa," the horse will slow down. Raising your voice slightly and speaking in a sharp tone can inform your horse that he is being naughty.

Artificial Aids

Artificial aids such as crops or spurs help the natural aids.

Crops: Crops are meant to give your leg extra oomph. If your horse is lazy or ignoring your leg, you may need to use a crop. There are several kinds of crops to choose from including short jumping bats, medium-sized crops, and long

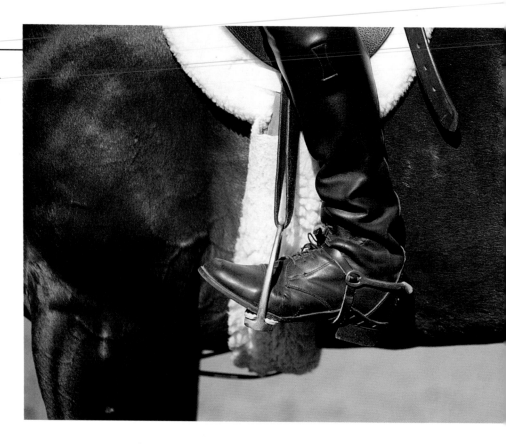

Spurs give your legs extra oomph.

dressage whips. Most horse people carry the whip in their inside hand to stop a horse from cutting corners, but you may need to switch over to the outside hand for training reasons. While holding the reins, hold the handle of the crop in your palm and let the bottom part rest on your thigh.

Some crops have a wrist loop, but don't slip your hand through it. If the crop gets caught on something you could injure your hand, which is why some people cut off these loops.

Use a crop as little as possible and only if a horse has ignored your natural aids such as your legs or voice. If he ignores your legs, use the whip on his side, directly behind your leg. Put your reins in one hand and use the crop hand to reach back and give him one or two smart smacks. Then continue your work. If you are using a short crop, hold the reins with one hand and use the other to give your horse a whack behind your leg. Don't hold the rein and whack your horse on the

shoulder with the same hand because you will yank him in the mouth. Most of your horse's power comes from his back end, so hitting him on the shoulder is fairly ineffective. Experts recommend a tap behind your leg, on his side.

A dressage whip is about 3 feet long, and you can use it without taking your hand off the rein. Turn your wrist and tap the whip across your thigh so the tip of the whip taps your horse behind your leg. A dressage whip stings more than a regular crop so don't use it with too much force.

Never lose your temper and beat your horse with a crop, and never use one on his head. It can frighten him and make him head shy (afraid of having his head touched).

Spurs: Spurs also give your legs extra power because most horses react when pointy metal objects are pressed into their sides! (Who

At the walk, follow the bobbing movement of your horse's head with your hands.

wouldn't react?) If you are new to riding, do not wear spurs right away. First learn to use your legs correctly before strapping on a pair of spurs. New riders often jab their horses with spurs unnecessarily.

Spurs should be blunt and short. Prince of Wales spurs are very popular with English-style riders. They are about ½ inch long. Some boots have spur rests so you know where the spurs should be worn. Otherwise they should be just under your anklebone. Make sure they are level or slanting down.

If your horse is poking along, use your calf muscles first to get his attention. If he doesn't react to them, turn your toe out and give him a quick nudge with the spurs. Then return your lower leg to the correct position.

Try not to kick your horse with spurs in anger. Some horses have scars on their sides thanks to rough riders wearing sharp spurs.

FIRST STEPS

Once you are mounted, check your position before you set off at the walk. Think about how you look. Are your legs slightly behind the girth? Are you sitting up straight? Are your hands parallel to each other and close to the withers? Are your reins even? You may have to shorten them.

When you're ready, look straight ahead and squeeze your horse's sides with both of your lower legs. He should walk forward. If he does, stop giving him the leg aid as a reward for moving forward. Then keep your leg quietly touching his side. If he doesn't move, squeeze him several times. If he still doesn't step forward, it's time for a tap of the whip behind your leg. Don't hesitate—you are the boss!

When your horse is walking, keep your legs touching his sides. If he is obedient and moving forward, you don't have to keep squeezing.

Simply keep your leg on him. Then concentrate on keeping your heels down and pointing your toes straight ahead.

At first, your instructor will probably tell you to use a fairly loose rein. This is to prevent your pulling on the horse's mouth if you suddenly lose your balance. As you become more secure in the saddle, you will get used to your horse's movement as he walks forward. As he moves, he nods his head. You'll feel this motion with your hands through the reins. Keep your hands soft and flexible and try to let them follow the movement of the horse's head. Imagine that the reins are rubber bands, and let your hands give and take with the pressure. This is called "having contact."

When an instructor tells you to "take up contact with the reins," that means shorten your reins so you can follow the motion of your horse's head. It is important to get used to the way good contact feels. If your reins are too tight, your horse will think you want him to stop, but if the reins are too loose, you'll have little control over your horse, making it difficult to turn or stop.

Sometimes it's difficult to get a lazy horse to move. Riding-school horses are often particularly tough to get going! But should you kick a horse who won't move? Some instructors say yes, but too much kicking can upset a horse and deaden his sides forever.

If you ride a slowpoke, use short, sharp squeezes from your lower legs. Little kicks may work too. Once he is moving, squeeze him with alternate legs to keep him going; in other words, squeeze once with your left leg, then, as he steps forward, squeeze him with your right leg.

STEERING

Once your horse is walking forward nicely, it won't be long before you have to turn him. When you are first learning to steer, it may seem natural to pull on the rein in the direction you want to go. But pulling looks bad, and it isn't the most effective way to turn a horse. Use both your hands and legs to steer.

Before you make your turn, look in the direction you want to go, then ask your horse to turn. If you're turning left, use your fingers to squeeze the left rein. Pull your hand back a tiny bit. Your horse should turn his head slightly to the left. You should be able to see his eye.

Your right hand should be close to his neck, and you should keep a steady, but soft, feel on the right rein. If he doesn't turn his head, you may have to tug gently on the left rein

Squeeze on the rein to ask your horse to turn.

several times to get his attention. Reward him when he turns his head by not tugging anymore, and by softening your hold on the rein. At the same time, keep your left leg near the girth and move your right leg back a bit, behind the girth. These are the aids that tell your horse to bend his body when he turns. He should bend his body around your left leg. Your right leg, behind the girth, prevents him from swinging his hindquarters around and straightening up. Once you have turned, stop squeezing on the left rein and move your right leg back to the girth. Now your horse can straighten up again.

Keep your outside leg behind the girth when turning.

Don't lift your hand in the air when asking your horse to turn.

To turn to the right, squeeze the right rein until he turns his head slightly. Keep your right leg next to the girth and your left leg behind the girth. If you are riding in a circle, think "inside leg next to the girth, outside leg behind the girth" and your horse should bend to the turn without a fuss.

Turning Tips

Always look in the direction you want your horse to go. Turning your head slightly shifts your body weight and affects your balance. Even a quiet, or tiny, movement tells your horse you want him to turn.

Don't lean too much or put too much weight in one stirrup. This can unbalance your horse and make the turn look and feel clumsy.

Don't lift the turning hand up in the air. Keep your hands close together. Your movements should be subtle. A spectator should not be able to tell that you're asking for a turn.

Changing Direction

Before long, your instructor will ask you to change direction. There are several easy ways to do this. Wait until you reach the middle of the long side of the ring and turn your horse inward. Walk across the middle of the ring; then turn right when you get near the rail.

You could also do a half turn, sometimes called a half circle. Simply turn your horse to the inside, make a small 10- to 20-meter loop, head off in the other direction, and return to the rail.

STOPPING

Prepare yourself to halt before you give your horse any instructions. Sit deeply in the saddle on both of your seat bones. Keep your back straight, and look ahead to where you want your horse to halt. Don't take your legs off his sides.

To begin to halt, keep your legs on his sides, but stop squeezing with them. Now, stop following the horse's movement with your hands and start squeezing your fingers around the reins. Doing this puts pressure on the horse's bit and tells him to slow down. A few horses listen to voice commands and it may help to say "whoa." Continue squeezing the reins until he stops. When he halts, relax your hands and stop squeezing immediately. This is very important. You must reward a horse who stops by releasing your hold on his mouth.

It may seem easier to halt a horse by pulling back on both reins at the same time. You've probably seen many riders do this, but it doesn't always stop a horse. In fact, many horses fight against a constant hold, and they may pull against you even more. Small tugs or squeezes on the reins are usually more effective than constant pulling. As with turning, asking your horse to halt should be a quiet motion. Too often, people are rough with their hands when they ask a horse to stop; rough hands often make a horse resist and throw his head in the air.

Some disobedient horses pull against you no matter what you do. In this case, you need to be more aggressive in the saddle. Lift your hands up slightly and give several quick pulls on the horse's mouth until he stops.

Once you can stop your horse effectively, try to get him to stand square. This means he halts with his front and hind legs lined up evenly. His head, neck, and back should be straight, and he should have his weight on all four legs. Getting a square halt takes time and practice. If he doesn't halt squarely the first time, nudge him forward a step or two until he stands properly. Ask a friend to draw a line in the dirt, and try to get your horse to halt with his front legs standing on the line.

Practice halting every time you ride. Ask for the halt while you are walking along a line and your horse's body is straight. Some horses fidget and move around when you ask them to halt. If yours does this, ask him to halt for only a second or two, then let him walk forward in a straight line. Try to increase the amount of time he stands quietly. Praise him and give him a pat on the neck when he stands still.

Next, ask him to stand for several minutes while you chat with a friend or watch an ongoing lesson. Don't forget about your position when your horse stands quietly. Sit straight in the saddle. Don't get lazy and slouch just because your horse isn't moving forward.

There may come a time when he will have to stand quietly. At shows, for example, you'll have to line up and stand still during classes, and a judge will take points off a fidgety horse. You may also need him to stand still to let cars pass before crossing a busy street, or on a trail to let other horses or a rattlesnake pass by.

If your horse refuses to stand still, you may have to work on halting him from the ground. Lead him around in his bridle and ask him to halt from the ground, using your voice and tugs on the reins.

Try to get your horse to halt squarely.

MASTERING THE TROT

ONCE YOU CAN WALK, TURN, AND STOP A horse effectively, it's time to trot. Now, trotting can seem very bumpy and fast after the nice, smooth walk. The first time you trot, you may find yourself bouncing around on the saddle and grabbing onto your horse's mane so you don't fall off. Don't panic. You'll soon get used to the up-and-down motion.

One of the best ways to learn how to trot is to start out on a lunge line. In your lessons, ask your instructor to lunge you while you get used to the bumpiness of the trot. This way, you can concentrate on keeping your balance while your instructor controls the horse. At first, trot for only one or two minutes at a time. You'll find that staying secure in the saddle requires a lot of effort and you'll be using muscles you probably haven't used before!

Your horse should be walking energetically before you ask for the trot.

Squeeze with your lower legs to ask your horse to trot.

Your position at the trot should be the same as at the walk:

🐎 Look in the direction you're going.

🐎 Keep your elbows close to your body.

🐎 Keep your hands even and near your horse's withers.

🐎 Sit up and keep your back straight.

🐎 Sit deep in the saddle and distribute your weight evenly on both seat bones.

🐎 Keep your lower legs glued to your horse's sides.

Before you ask for the trot, make sure your horse is walking at a brisk pace. If she is poking along, it will take longer for her to begin trotting. Loosen your reins slightly, but hold on to the pommel of the saddle or a neck strap so your hands don't bounce up and down and yank your horse in her mouth, which can hurt and annoy her, too. Pulling on her mouth also tells her that you want to halt, which is not what you want at this time.

TIME TO TROT

Once your position is perfect, and your horse is walking smoothly, squeeze with your legs—as you did to get her walking—and your horse should begin trotting. If she doesn't trot right away, squeeze again and again. If she ignores you, give a little nudge or kick. If she still won't trot, tap her behind your lower leg with a crop. Your goal is to get your horse to trot immediately. Don't let her dillydally. Once she's trotting, you want her to move forward at a brisk, steady pace. Her steps should be regular and even. When you're used to trotting, shorten the reins slightly for more control over your horse's speed and direction.

Try to relax at the trot. Take deep breaths and loosen up. A relaxed body absorbs the up-and-down motion. A stiff, tense body bounces around, which is painful for both horse and rider. Sit deep in the saddle. Don't lean forward over your horse's neck and grip with your knees. That puts your rear end out of the saddle so you won't be bumping it, but your leaning forward isn't comfortable for your horse and makes it difficult for you to keep your balance. If your horse stumbles while you're leaning forward, you can take a dive. Leaning forward also tells your horse to go faster. That's not what you want when you're learning to trot!

TRANSITIONS

During lessons, you may hear your instructor talk about transitions. A transition is simply a change of gait or pace. Going from walk to trot is a transition; so is going from a trot to canter. An upward transition means going from a slower gait to a faster gait. A downward transition means going from a faster gait to a slower gait.

Ask for upward transitions by squeezing or nudging your horse with your legs. Loosen your reins slightly so you don't pull your horse in the mouth when she shifts up a gear. When you ask for downward transitions, sit deep in the saddle and push your shoulders back. Keep your legs on your horse's sides without squeezing them and squeeze the reins with your fingers. As soon as your horse slows down, reward her by loosening your hold on her mouth.

Your goal as a rider is to make transitions as smooth as possible. When you ask your horse to trot, she should trot right away. It shouldn't take three minutes of kicking to get her going. And when you ask for the walk from the trot, you shouldn't have to pull hard on the reins to get her to slow down. A downward transition should take a few steps at most.

If your horse is well balanced when you ask for a transition, she shouldn't have a problem slowing down or speeding up smoothly. But if she is slopping along with her nose on the ground—or high-stepping with her head in the air—your transitions will be messy. Organize and settle your horse before you ask for a transition.

POSTING (RISING) TROT

Trotting will seem a lot smoother once you learn the posting, or rising, trot. Posting means rising up and down in the saddle as your horse trots along. It lessens the stress on your horse's back and makes trotting less tiring for you both.

When your horse trots, she springs from one diagonal pair of legs to the other. For example, her front right leg and her back left leg move forward at the same time. Then the front left leg and back right leg move forward together. There is a moment of suspension between each step. This is why the trot is so bouncy.

When you post, you rise out of the saddle when one diagonal pair of legs lifts off the ground, and sit down as the same pair returns to the ground. You'll soon notice that the natural movement of your horse actually bounces you forward and slightly out of the saddle, making posting fairly easy. Try to stay close to the saddle, though. Some extra-springy horses can bounce you too high, making your riding style less than efficient!

Trotting is a two-beat gait and posting will come easier if you count "one-two" as your horse moves along. (Rise on "one" and sit on "two.") Count to yourself until you start feeling a rhythm, then start rising and sitting in time to the horse's trot.

Practice posting while your horse is walking or standing still. As you rise, push down on the stirrups with the balls of your feet. Then slowly sink back into the saddle.

Rise out of the saddle when the outside hoof is forward.

Sit in the saddle when the outside hoof is under your horse.

DIAGONALS

Once you can post the trot, you must master diagonals. Diagonals are a way of making sure you are up out of the saddle—or sitting down in the saddle—on the correct beat. The diagonal you should be on depends on which direction your horse is traveling in an arena. If you are on the correct diagonal, it is easier for your horse to stay balanced as she trots around the arena.

If you are riding around the ring on the right rein (your right hand is on the inside), you should rise and sit in time with your horse's left foreleg—the front one on the outside of the arena. If you are riding on the left rein (your left hand is on the inside), you should rise and sit in time with your horse's right foreleg.

Checking Your Diagonal

While you are trotting during a lesson, your instructor may call, "Check your diagonal!" This usually means you are on the incorrect one. There is an easy way to tell if you're on the correct diagonal. Lower your eyes only (not your head—this affects your balance) and look at your horse's outside foreleg. When it is forward, you should be up in the air. When it is back, you should be sitting in the saddle.

When you change direction, change your diagonal, too. This is simple. As you change direction, sit in the saddle for two beats, then rise again. Think to yourself: "Up-down, up-down, down-up." You should be on the correct diagonal. If you aren't, sit down another two beats, then rise.

It is important to be on the correct diagonal when you're competing in a flat class at a show (one in which you walk, trot, and canter). Being on the wrong diagonal could knock you out of the ribbons.

Out of the Ring

If you're on a trail ride and there is no inside or outside rein, change your diagonal every once in a while. This keeps your horse flexible; she won't get too used to one diagonal.

Some horses are more comfortable to ride on one diagonal than the other, but you must force yourself to change diagonals regularly, for your horse's sake.

Alternate diagonals when riding outside of the ring.

SITTING TROT

The sitting trot is a great way of improving your balance on a horse. It also strengthens your leg and seat muscles. But it can be tiring for both you and your horse, so practice it for only short periods until you can do it properly.

You don't rise when you do the sitting trot. Sit deep in the saddle and keep your back straight. Push your shoulders back. Keep your thighs close against the saddle flap, but don't grip with them. This only makes you bounce more. Stretch your legs down and keep them close to your horse's sides. When you first try the sitting trot, you may need to hold on to the pommel with one hand to stop bouncing.

Remember to relax while you sit the trot, and try to let your body absorb the bumpy motion.

Try to relax when doing a sitting trot.

TROTTING EXERCISES

Here are some easy exercises to work on while schooling your horse:

Circles: Do a lot of circles at the trot. They make your horse supple. Make sure they're round, not lumpy. Do them in the corners of the arena and in the middle. Try to keep your horse's body bent around your inside leg. You should be able to see her inside eye.

Changes of Direction: Change your direction by riding down the center of the arena or cutting across the middle. You can also do half turns (half circles) at the trot.

Transitions: Go from walk to trot, trot to walk, trot to halt, etc. Keep your horse thinking and alert at all times!

Serpentines: Do serpentines, large S-shaped figures, up and down the arena. Keep your loops even.

Figure Eights: Practice figure eights at the trot. Make sure both circles are round and the same size. Remember to change your diagonal when you change directions.

Leg Yielding: This exercise teaches a horse to obey your leg aids. Try it on the track on the long side of the arena. Make sure your horse's body is straight as you trot on. Then squeeze with your outside leg and ask your horse to move away from the pressure. She should move forward and sideways at the same time. After she moves sideways for a few steps, let her go forward for a second or two, then use your other leg to ask her to move back to the track again.

Doing circles at the trot can make your horse more supple.

*Give your horse
a lot of praise when
he performs well.*

PRAISE AND REWARDS

Always remember to praise your horse during a schooling session. If she performs a movement well, pat her on her neck with your hand and praise her verbally. Horses know the difference between praise and punishment.

Reward your horse by letting her relax occasionally. Loosen your hold on the reins and walk around the ring. Some people reward their horses with sugar cubes or horse treats, but horses can get used to this and start to expect tasty treats in the middle of a schooling session. Plus, sugar isn't great for your horse's teeth. It's better to give your horse a treat such as an apple or some carrots when you're done riding.

If your horse is being naughty, don't hesitate to punish her quickly. If she is being sluggish or stubborn, tap her with a whip to get her moving. If she ignores other aids, sometimes a growl or a sharp verbal "no!" can make a horse focus on the task at hand. You will have to see what works for you and your horse and stick with it. Never lose your temper and beat a horse. One or two hard smacks on her hindquarters and a stern "no" are enough.

Always discipline your horse immediately if she displays dangerous behavior such as kicking or biting. Don't wait several minutes because by then she won't remember what she is being punished for!

TROTTING WITHOUT STIRRUPS

Riding without stirrups is a great way to strengthen your leg muscles so you can use them more effectively. It also teaches you how to sit properly on both of your seat bones and develop a secure seat, instead of relying on your stirrups so much.

If you "lose a stirrup" (your foot slips out of the stirrup iron) during a lesson, or while competing in a show, it is important to keep going without losing your balance. You shouldn't stop your horse and pick up your iron again. It wastes time and you might lose points in a show. So don't cringe or whine during your lesson the next time your instructor tells you to "drop 'em!" It's good practice.

You should set out to ride without stirrups at least once or twice a week. You don't have to do it for long. Twenty minutes is fine because at first you'll bump around a lot, and this won't be very pleasant for you or your horse. When you get better at riding without stirrups, you can do it longer.

If you are going to ride without stirrups for a while, secure them by crossing them over the saddle in front of you so they don't fly around and bang your horse's sides. Pull both stirrups down a bit so the buckle is about three inches away from the stirrup bar. (Pulling the buckle down helps the leathers lie flat so they don't rub your legs.) Then, cross them over your horse's neck and rest them on either side of her withers.

Before you pick up the trot, let your legs hang down under you. They should touch your horse's sides. Keep your toes pointing forward and your heels lower than your toes. Sit deep so both seat bones touch the saddle. Sit up straight and push out your chest. Keep your elbows close to your sides and your hands close together. Squeeze your horse forward into the trot.

Ride with fairly loose reins so you don't pull on your horse's mouth if you start to bump up and down. Breathe deeply, relax, and move with your horse.

Give posting without stirrups a go. Figure out which diagonal you're on, and start rising up and down. Push your legs close to your horse's sides and let your inner knees and lower thighs have a slight grip on the saddle. Let the horse's bouncy movement push you up and out of the saddle. When you sit down again, let your inner knee and lower thigh relax.

PICKING UP YOUR STIRRUPS

Practice dropping and picking up your stirrups at the trot without looking down or moving the stirrup leather with your hand. Begin by slipping your feet out of the stirrups, walking a few strides, and then putting your feet back in them. Once you can do this without looking down, try it at the trot and canter. Don't cheat and look down! This skill comes in handy when you're riding cross-country or at a show and don't have time to stop and pick up a lost stirrup.

*Trotting without stirrups is a great way
to strengthen your legs.*

The Canter

When you feel completely secure in the saddle at the trot, try cantering. The canter has a smoother pace, and the feeling is very pleasant—much like being in a rocking chair. When your horse canters, he seems to be rocking backward and forward in a rhythm, and so do you. During the canter, the sequence of footfalls is as follows: right hind, right diagonal pair, left leading fore, followed by a moment of suspension.

The canter is faster than the trot, so you must be in complete control of your horse before you ask him to speed up. It's a good idea to learn how to canter in an enclosed ring instead of out on a trail where your horse can run off with you.

When you are first learning to canter, it's best to ask for it from the trot. Experienced horses can pick up the canter from the walk but it is easier for them to start from the trot. It is easier for you, too, as your horse should already be moving forward at a brisk pace. He won't be able to pick up a canter nicely if he is poking along with his nose to the ground. Before you even ask for the canter, make sure your horse is actively trotting forward, especially along the long side of the arena. Get him balanced by making sure both reins are the same length and keeping both legs pressed on his sides.

If your horse is a bit lazy and difficult to keep trotting nicely, squeeze with both legs every time you rise. This should remind your horse that you want him to trot. Keep a soft but firm hold on his mouth and keep his head up. Concentrate on keeping your back straight and look ahead.

LEADS

Pick up the canter when your horse is trotting in a circle or around a bend in the arena because he is more likely to pick up the correct lead. What's a lead? When your horse canters, his inside foreleg should reach farther forward or step a bit higher than his outside foreleg. Instructors sometimes call the inside foreleg the leading leg. Your horse will be better balanced if he is on the correct lead.

ASKING FOR THE CANTER

When you reach a bend in the arena or while you are circling, work on getting your horse to bend around your inside leg. Place your inside leg next to the girth and your outside leg behind the girth. Squeeze the inside rein so he turns his head to the inside. You should be able to see his eye. Don't ask for the canter unless your horse

Your horse must be trotting actively before you ask for the canter.

You should be doing a sitting trot when you give the aids to canter.

is bending properly. His head and his hindquarters should be pointing slightly inward. Then you can give the following aids:

🐎 Stop rising to the trot and sit deep in the saddle.

🐎 Push your heels down and point your toes forward.

🐎 Place your outside leg behind the girth and give him a squeeze or a small kick.

If your horse doesn't canter, keep him bending and nudge him harder with your outside leg. If he still doesn't move out, it's crop time. Give him a smack right behind your outside leg and squeeze with the leg at the same time. If a horse ignores your aids, it's best to use a crop immediately behind your outside leg rather than continue to kick and kick and kick. Most horses respond quickly to a sharp tap from a crop.

When your horse takes off, it feels as if he's leaping into the air. Keep your legs firmly on his sides and glue your rear end to the saddle. Relax and try to follow your horse's rocking movement with your whole body.

Your horse's inside leg should lead at the canter.

Just as you do at the walk, let your hands and the reins follow the motion of your horse's head and neck. It's important that you don't pull him in the mouth every time he surges forward. You must always encourage your horse to move forward freely. Don't punish him by grabbing the reins and pulling him in the mouth.

If your horse canters off at top speed, let him continue forward for a stride or two before you bring him back by sitting deep in the saddle and squeezing both reins.

At first, you may not be able to tell if your horse is on the correct lead. You will have to look down and make sure his inside hoof is stretching out farther than his outside hoof. Don't tilt your whole head, though; this can throw off your balance. Simply lower your eyes. As you spend more and more time in the saddle, you'll be able to feel when your horse is on the wrong lead. Most horses feel slightly off balance and may be a bit stiff or move clumsily when they're on the wrong lead.

If your horse takes off on the wrong lead, immediately slow him down to a trot by squeezing on the reins and sitting back in the saddle. Don't rise. Sit the trot and ask for the canter again by squeezing on the inside rein and giving him a nudge with your outside leg behind the girth.

There is a moment of suspension at the canter when all four legs are in the air.

Don't tip your head to check if your horse is on the correct lead.

Relax and follow your horse's rocking movement with your body.

Cantering Tips

🐎 Don't lean to the inside when asking your horse to canter. This unbalances both of you and makes it hard for him to strike off on the correct leading leg.

🐎 If you can't get in sync with your horse's rocking motion, try to adjust your position quickly so you are moving with him. Sitting too far back makes your legs fly forward, and you won't be secure in the saddle. Bouncing around at the back of the saddle can also hurt your horse's back. Move slightly forward in the saddle and push your legs down underneath you.

🐎 Make sure you canter equally on both leading legs. Your horse may pick up one lead better than the other, or he may be more comfortable to ride on one lead. Don't get lazy. Work him in both directions during your schooling (training and exercising) sessions.

LEAD PROBLEMS

If you're having major problems getting your horse to pick up the correct lead, lunge him without a rider for a few days. If he has problems picking up the lead on the lunge line, he may have back or leg problems. If this seems to be the case, call the vet or horse chiropractor for an evaluation.

If he picks up the leads just fine on the lunge, you (the rider) are probably the problem! If your position is not spot-on, your horse may have difficulty getting balanced. Sign up for some lessons with a reputable instructor. After watching you and your horse in action, she may be able to suggest some training methods to conquer your lead problems.

If your horse picks up the correct lead when you lunge him, but not when you ride him—the problem could be you!

CANTERING EXERCISES

Circles: Do a lot of circles at the canter. Circles help a horse become supple. When you school your horse, include some increasing and decreasing circles. Start working in a small 10-meter circle, then gradually increase the size to 20 meters.

Figure Eights: Do large figure eights. Canter a circle in one direction, then bring your horse back to the trot at the center of the eight, and ask for the canter on the other leading leg, heading off in the other direction. Figure eights are a great way to help your horse learn how to pick up the correct lead.

Flying Lead Changes: A flying lead change is when a horse changes leading legs while he is

cantering. He does not have to slow down to the trot to change leading legs. As he leaps into the air, he shifts his weight from one side to the other and the other leg begins reaching out farther than the other. As you and your horse become more proficient about picking up the correct lead, you can attempt flying lead changes at the center of the eight where you change your direction.

A horse who can do flying lead changes is necessary for people who want to enter hunter classes over fences. Often, you need to change your horse's lead if you have to change direction in the middle of a course. Some horses change lead in midair over a fence if they are given the correct aids. If they don't get the change in the air, they must do it within two or three strides of landing on the other side of the fence. In some hunter classes, a judge will mark you down if your horse is traveling on the wrong lead around a course.

Flying lead changes take awhile to master. Riding figure eights is one way you can teach your horse to do them. Start by cantering on one lead, then come back to the trot at the center of the eight and ask with your normal cantering aids for the different leading leg. Strongly use your outside leg so he reacts to it quickly. Start decreasing the time you allow your horse to trot. Give him only a stride or two to change leads. Eventually your horse will learn to change his lead without coming back to the trot. He should recognize what your aids mean, and act upon them.

THE GALLOP

The horse's fastest speed is the gallop, and for most riders it is the most exciting gait. It's faster than the canter because the horse takes bigger strides. As he races along, he stretches out his head, neck, and body as far as he can.

Galloping is great fun, but it can be dangerous. It's very easy for a horse traveling at top speed to get out of control, especially if his rider is inexperienced. Some horses take advantage of you at the gallop and tear off wherever they want. Practice galloping in an enclosed ring before you try it out on a trail or in a big field. It is important that you are able to stop or slow down your horse at all times before you attempt galloping. Galloping is always dangerous on uneven ground.

Preparing to Gallop

Once your horse is cantering, shorten your reins a bit and start squeezing with your legs until he picks up speed. Push your heels down and lift your seat out of the saddle. Tilt your upper body slightly forward and push your chest closer to your horse's neck. This is the galloping position—what jockeys do on the racetrack. Most horses speed up when you take your weight off their back. Then urge your horse

forward by squeezing with your lower leg. You may have to give him a kick or two.

Move your hands a little higher up your horse's neck and let them follow the movement of his head as it stretches forward with each stride. Look straight ahead to make sure the path ahead is clear. When you want to slow down, sit back in the saddle and squeeze on both reins. Keep your lower legs on your horse's sides, but stop squeezing or kicking. When he slows down, reward his obedience by immediately loosening your hold on the reins.

Galloping Tips

Don't flap your arms and legs around while galloping. It may be great fun zipping along at top speed, but you shouldn't forget your position. Keep your elbows close to your body and glue your legs to your horse's sides.

Don't grip the saddle with your knees. If you do, your lower legs will automatically shoot back, and you'll lose your security in the saddle. If your horse bucks or stumbles, you could eat some dirt! Ouch!

The Hand Gallop

Show judges often ask competitors to hand gallop in flat classes. This is a controlled gallop. It is faster than a canter, but not quite a flat-out gallop. Judges usually ask you to hand gallop along the long side of the arena, and competitors are usually asked to do it one at a time. You must get up in galloping position, urge your horse to stretch out his neck, and move at a brisk pace. The judge expects to see plenty of energy so make sure your horse is putting some oomph into it!

When galloping, lean forward so your weight is off your horse's back.

CANTERING AND GALLOPING IN A GROUP

One of the best things about owning a horse is being able to ride in the open countryside with your friends. Before you charge off, however, remember that it's exciting for a horse to be in company, and he may behave differently in the open than he does in the ring. Even the quietest school horse may suddenly experience an extra burst of energy the second he steps out of the ring. You must be prepared for frisky or naughty behavior.

You may need stronger equipment on your horse if you plan to do fast work in the open. You may have to use a twisted snaffle instead of a plain snaffle, and a martingale will probably come in handy.

Keep a safe distance away from the other riders, but try not to let them get too far ahead. This will upset your horse, and he'll want to run to catch up. If you're riding with several people, try to keep your position in the group. Don't zoom past the front rider—you could make her horse misbehave.

Most important, communicate with the other riders in the group before you take off. Decide as a group that you're going to canter or gallop. Don't zip off without warning. Give yourselves time to tighten your hold on the reins and make sure your position is secure. Once you set off, pay attention to the rest of the bunch. If someone is having problems controlling his horse, it's best if everybody slows down until he is in control again. There is always the danger of the horses bolting as a group.

Chapter Six

Jumping

IT WILL PROBABLY TAKE A FEW MONTHS OF walking, trotting, and cantering before you're ready to start jumping. Why? Because you must be perfectly balanced and safe on your horse's back before you pop over fences. When a horse jumps, she leaps into the air, and if you're not 100 percent secure on her back, you could fall off or hinder her as she jumps. You also need to have complete control over your horse on the flat before you start jumping. You must know how to slow down or speed up instantly, and you must be able to stop and turn her easily. If you can't control your horse on the flat, it's unlikely that jumping will be safe or enjoyable.

Begin your jumping career by starting small. Trotting over poles may seem boring, but it prepares you for jumping bigger fences later on.

Before starting, shorten your stirrups one or two holes. Shorter stirrups help bring your body weight forward so that you can stay over your horse's center of balance throughout her jump. This makes jumping easier for her. Keep your feet in the stirrups while you shorten them.

*Shorten your stirrups
before jumping.*

JUMPING POSITION

Before you jump your first pole, you need to know how to get into the jumping position, sometimes called the two-point position or the

Practice the jumping position while working on the flat.

Let's take a look at the correct jumping position.

half seat. In the jumping position, you lean forward over your horse's neck and lift your rear end slightly out of the saddle. Sitting forward helps you stay balanced and allows you to move with your horse as she clears a fence. It's not easy for her to jump if you are bouncing around on her back and making her unbalanced. It's hard enough for a horse to clear a fence—don't make it more difficult!

Head: Hold your head high and keep your eyes up. Looking down affects your balance in the saddle and, in turn, can affect your horse's balance.

Shoulders: Don't slouch. Push your shoulders back and down. If you're lucky enough to have a mirror in the arena, check your position. Your shoulders should be in line with or slightly in front of your knees.

Upper Body: Bend your upper body forward from your hips, not your waist, over your horse's neck. Stick your chest out a bit. Keep your back flat and straight, not rounded and hunched over.

Seat: Push your seat backward and lift it slightly out of the saddle. Your rear end should be close enough so that you can sit down quickly and get back into your regular riding position.

Thighs: Keep your thighs close to the saddle. Bend your knees and let your thighs touch the saddle flap.

Lower Legs: Your lower legs should be underneath you, close to the girth. Keep a strong hold on your horse's sides so you can ask her to move forward. Your legs must stay glued in this position, even when you're flying over a fence. Look down at your stirrup leathers. They should be straight up and down, not positioned at an angle. Keep your ankles flexible. They are shock absorbers for the rest of your body.

Feet: Place the ball of your foot (the widest part) on the stirrup tread, and push your heels down lower than your toes. Try to keep your toes pointing forward, but it's okay if they stick out to the side a little.

Arms: Push your arms forward so your elbows are in front of your body instead of glued to your sides, as they are when you're doing flatwork. Bend your arms at the elbows, and imagine a straight line from your elbows all the way down your arms and the reins to your horse's mouth.

Hands: Keep your hands level and as close together as possible. They should be near your horse's neck or withers. Face your thumbs upward at all times.

Maintain a firm grip on the reins by keeping your fingers closed. Shorten your reins slightly, but continue to follow the forward motion of your horse's head and neck. Practice your jumping position at the walk, trot, and canter. Stay in the position for a few minutes, then sit down and rest. The jumping position is tiring. When you do it properly, your leg muscles get a real workout.

Hang On!

If you have trouble keeping your balance when you practice the jumping position, here are three tips—one of which you may find useful:

1. Place your palms on the sides of your horse's neck, near the top, and press down.

2. Grab hold of some mane.

3. Use a neckstrap to stop yourself from bouncing around. Fasten a stirrup leather around your horse's neck like a collar (not too tight) and hold on to it.

If you lose your balance, it's better to hold on to a neck strap or mane than to grab the reins and yank on your horse's mouth. As you become a better (and stronger) rider, you'll be able to maintain the jumping position without these helpful aids.

THE RELEASE

Once you start jumping, it's very important that you learn how to temporarily loosen your hold on the reins and your horse's mouth. This is often called a release or a quick release.

As your horse jumps over a fence, she stretches out her head and neck. If you have a strong hold on the reins, you could jab her in the mouth. This can be painful, as well as confusing to your horse. She's jumping the fence as you've asked her to, yet you are punishing her by hurting her mouth. Right from the start, learn how to use a release.

A release is when you push your hands forward as you're about to jump over a pole or a fence. Rest your hands on your horse's neck, about 8 to 10 inches in front of the saddle. This loosens the reins slightly and there's less chance of hurting your horse's mouth.

Also, when you push your hands forward, grab hold of some mane. This helps you maintain a good release over a fence.

TROTTING POLES

You may want to jump a fence right away, but it's best to start small and build up your confidence. Trotting over poles gives you time to practice your jumping position and improve your balance. Use white or colored trotting poles. Natural-colored ones can be difficult for a horse to see.

Use at least four or five trotting poles and place them parallel to each other across your path. Never use only two because an enthusiastic horse may try to jump both of them at the same time.

It is important to set up the trotting poles the correct distance apart on the ground. The distance you set them apart depends on the size of the horse you are riding. A pony's stride is naturally smaller than a horse's, so you must place trotting poles for a pony closer together than you would if you were riding a horse. A small pony will have a hard time trotting nicely over poles spaced for a horse, and a big horse may trip over poles set for a pony. Following is a rough guide to setting up trotting poles. You may need to adjust the distances to suit your own horse, but these measurements give you a starting point.

Begin by trotting over poles on the ground.

Pony Poles: If you ride a pony, place the poles about 3½ to 4 feet (1.2m) apart. If they're farther apart, the pony may stumble.

Horse Poles: If you ride a horse, place the poles about 4½ to 5 feet (1.5m) apart. These distances may need to be adjusted, depending on the size of your horse's stride.

Once the poles are set, ask your horse to trot around the ring at a steady, active pace. She should pick up her feet and not poke along.

Squeeze with your lower legs each time you rise out of the saddle.

When she is moving nicely, get into the jumping position. Then give yourself plenty of room to approach the poles and head for them in a straight line. Don't yank your horse into them at the last second. Steer her toward the middle of the poles. As she approaches the first one, do a release so you don't jab her in the mouth as she stretches her head forward.

Your first jump should be a small cross-pole placed after the trotting poles.

Here are some things to think about when going over the poles:

Keep your horse moving at a steady pace all the way through the poles. If she slows down, squeeze with your lower legs or give her a quick nudge with your heels. Having a lot of energy is known as "impulsion," and your horse needs it to jump over a fence.

If she speeds up too much, sit back in the saddle and rise to the trot over the poles. Squeeze the reins with your fingers to slow her down.

Keep your horse in the middle of the poles. If she veers to the right, push her back over by pressing her right side with your right leg and squeezing on the opposite rein. If she veers to the left, push her over with your left leg and squeeze with the right rein. Don't just pull on the rein. Use your legs, too.

Look straight ahead.

Keep trotting forward after the last pole. Don't let your horse be lazy and stop.

Trot over the poles in both directions so your horse doesn't get bored.

When you have trotted over the last pole, sit back in the saddle, bring your hands back to their original position, and take up contact on the reins. Begin rising again.

Aim for the center of the fence.

YOUR FIRST JUMP

Your first jump should be a small cross-rail about three yards after a line of trotting poles. The fence should be only about 1½ feet off the ground. Popping over this low fence should be easy. You have time while you are trotting over the poles to get your jumping position in order. Also, your horse should be moving forward in a nice, active rhythm over the poles, so it will be easy for her to jump the fence.

As you head toward the poles, you must remember to:

Get into jumping position.

Push your hands forward in a release, and grab some mane.

Push your heels down and keep your legs close to your horse's sides.

Look straight ahead at the cross-rail fence and trot over the middle of the poles.

When you're finished with the trotting poles, stay in jumping position and steer your horse into the middle of the cross-rail fence. She should jump the center where the poles cross. Keep your legs glued to your horse's sides and squeeze to ask her to move forward.

When you are safely on the other side of the fence, continue riding in a straight line. Don't let your horse slow down or turn. Sit back in the saddle and take up your normal riding position.

When you feel confident, jump a single fence.

A SINGLE FENCE

The next fence to try is a small, simple vertical. Place one pole about 2 feet off the ground with a second pole on the ground about 8 to 10 inches in front of it. The ground pole helps a horse figure out where she should take off.

It may be difficult to keep your horse moving forward at a nice pace without the trotting poles, so get her listening to your legs before you head toward the fence. Circle once or twice before approaching the fence to give yourself some time

to get your horse trotting with plenty of impulsion. Now aim her for the center of the fence. Get into jumping position a few yards in front of the fence and grab some mane. Push your heels down and squeeze with your lower leg. Don't panic if your horse picks up a canter. If she is a few yards before the fence, sit back down and ask her to trot again. If she is very close to the fence, allow her to canter the last stride or two. Don't pull on her mouth to slow her down right in front of the fence. Let her think "forward," not "backward!"

When your horse lands, keep your legs glued to her sides, but don't squeeze. Sit back down in the saddle after a few strides, bring her back to the trot if she is cantering, and head toward the arena fence. Don't let your horse dart right or left immediately after the jump. Once you reach the arena fence, turn right or left or halt. If you're jumping the same fence several times, vary what you do on the landing side so your horse doesn't get bored.

You will soon notice that most horses jump smoothly when they take off about 3 feet away from the base of the jump. They take off at this spot if they're allowed to, but an unbalanced or rough rider can throw a horse off. She may get too close to the fence, take a tiny stride, and pop over it awkwardly. She can just as easily take off too far away from a fence and make a huge jump in the air. As you become a better rider, you will be able to adjust your horse's strides so she takes off at the right spot most of the time.

Always give your horse a big pat on the neck if she's done a good job.

A LINE

Once you can trot over one fence safely, try two. Set up another cross-rail about 60 feet after the first one. This is called a line. The large space between the two fences gives you plenty of time to land, regain control, and aim for the second one. Look at the second fence as you approach the first. If your horse canters after the first fence, sit back in the saddle and ask her to trot. As you become more experienced, you will canter to the second fence.

After jumping the first fence in a line, look ahead to the second.

JUMPING SMALL COURSES

When single fences are combined with lines in an arena, you have a course. Jumping a course is a challenge because you have to think ahead. As you approach one fence, you must think about and prepare for the next one. You have to know where it is, and how you are going to get there. You must also think about keeping a uniform pace throughout the course.

Memorize the course before you start, then pick up the trot and make sure you are on the correct diagonal. Do a large circle to establish your pace, then head for the middle of the first fence. Get into jumping position right in front of the fence, and sit back in the saddle when all four of your horse's feet are on the ground again. Rise to the trot between fences, and make sure you are on the correct diagonal. Utilize the whole arena when jumping a course. Don't cut corners. Take your time, and use corners to balance your horse and work on your position.

After you jump the last fence, make another big circle and slow down to the walk.

CANTERING FENCES

Learn how to canter over fences by jumping a line. Jump the first fence at a trot, then sit down in the saddle after your horse lands and ask for the canter. Some horses automatically pick up the canter after a jump. Squeeze with your legs to keep her cantering and look toward and over the second fence. Take a firm hold on the reins so your horse does not speed up. As you approach the second fence, get into jumping position and release with your hands. After you land, squeeze with your legs so your horse continues cantering. (Lazy horses will try to slow down.) Once you have mastered this exercise, you can canter over both fences in the line (and then try some single fences too).

Now try cantering over both fences in a line. Pick up a canter and ride in a big circle. Concentrate on getting your horse moving in a steady rhythm. Counting her strides out loud can help you keep an even pace. Give yourself plenty of room to approach the first fence and once you have landed start counting your strides.

Most instructors set the two fences in a line a specific amount of strides apart. Four or five is the norm. Lines are often 60 or 72 feet for horses, and 40 or 51 feet for ponies. Instructors usually set up lines based on the knowledge that the average horse's stride is about 12 feet long. If a line is 60 feet, most horses should easily jump it in five strides.

As you become more experienced, you will be able to control your horse's stride through a line at the canter. If the line is set for five strides, your instructor may ask you to speed up and stretch out your horse's stride so she jumps it in four. Or she may ask you to slow her down and shorten her stride so she jumps the line in six. These exercises help you develop an eye for distances. Soon you will be able to tell your horse how many strides to take in a line so she can take off at just the right spot in front of a fence and jump it in great style.

CANTERING AROUND A COURSE

First, you must figure out which lead you need to be on when you begin the course. Trot in a large circle in front of the first fence and pick up the correct lead, then canter around the same circle once before you aim your horse at the fence. This is often called a hunter circle, and it's your chance to get your horse cantering at a steady pace before you begin jumping.

As you become more experienced, you'll notice that most courses contain changes of

A refusal is when a horse stops in front of a fence.

direction. You may jump a fence on the left lead, and then have to pick up the right lead after you land. If you have an experienced horse, you could ask for a flying lead change in the air over the fence, or a stride or two after you land. If you're still learning, bring your horse back to the trot after a fence, then ask for the lead change.

JUMPING PROBLEMS

Several things can go wrong when jumping. Let's look at some typical situations.

Refusals

A refusal means that a horse doesn't want to jump a fence and stops in front of it. Sometimes the rider carries on over the fence alone! There are several reasons why a horse may refuse:

She may not have jumped much and is confused or scared. It may be necessary to go back to the basics with her for a while to restore her confidence. Stick to trotting poles and low fences until she jumps willingly.

She is being naughty or stubborn. Some horses won't jump unless their riders are giving them strong and effective aids. If you think your horse is plain-old misbehaving, carry a whip and give her a sharp tap behind your leg when she stops.

You are not secure in the saddle. A rider flopping around on a horse's back, unbalancing her and making it hard for her to jump, causes most refusals.

You are nervous. A horse can tell if you're scared. If she senses that you don't want to jump, she may not want to jump either. You need to be brave (or pretend to be!) when jumping.

Use a lot of leg on a horse who refuses. Sit deep in the saddle, and ask her to move on with your legs. Get into jumping position right in front of the fence, and squeeze with your legs to tell your horse to take off. Be firm—not wishy-washy—when riding a refuser.

Run-Outs

Sometimes a horse runs out to one side of a fence to avoid having to jump. If your horse tries to do this, take a strong contact on the reins when approaching a fence. Always steer her toward the middle of the fence, and squeeze strongly with your legs.

If your horse darts to the right, use a strong left rein and push her over with your right leg. If she nips to the left, tug on the right rein and push her over with your left leg.

Jumping to One Side

Always steer your horse to the center of the fence. Don't allow her to swerve to one side at the last second because she might run out.

Looking Down

Don't look down when jumping. This unbalances your horse and causes problems when you land because you aren't paying attention to where you're heading. Look straight ahead or toward your next fence.

Getting Left Behind

If you don't stay with your horse's motion as she jumps and have a lot of air between you and the saddle, you've been left behind. This isn't very comfortable for you or your horse because you will land back in the saddle with a big bump.

You may get left behind if you're not in jumping position when your horse takes off or if she jumps extra big over a small fence. If you get left behind a lot, hold on to the mane or a neck strap.

Ducking

Ducking is when a rider leans to one side when jumping a fence. It's a terrible habit that unbalances your horse. If your instructor tells you that you duck, you must concentrate on folding your body over your horse's neck and looking through her ears over a fence.

Try not to duck to one side when jumping.

Leaning too Far Forward

In our eagerness to jump, sometimes we throw ourselves over a fence before our horse has a chance to leave the ground! Leaning too forward causes your lower legs to slide back and your heels to pop up. If your horse refuses while you are in this insecure position, you'll fly over her head.

When approaching a fence, push your heels down, set your legs next to the girth, and keep your bottom close to the saddle. Instead of anticipating your horse's take-off point, relax and let the fence come to you.

Chapter Seven

Horse Problems

Very few horses are 100 percent perfectly behaved. Like people, horses often have a bad habit or two. Some horse habits such as sneaking mouthfuls of tasty grass are not too serious. But others such as bolting or rearing are dangerous and could cause injury to you or your horse.

REASONS FOR BAD BEHAVIOR

If your horse is normally well behaved but suddenly develops an annoying habit, don't panic.

You may be able to solve the problem by yourself. First, figure out why your horse is acting the way he is; then try changing his behavior. There are several reasons a horse behaves badly.

His tack doesn't fit properly: If his saddle is pinching his withers or rubbing his back, your horse will be unhappy and may buck or rear. If the underside of your saddle is lumpy and hard, your horse could be in pain. If his bit is too low, it may bang against his teeth and upset him. Check your tack thoroughly to make sure it fits your horse properly.

If your horse misbehaves, make sure his tack isn't hurting him.

He is unwell: A sick horse may be unwilling to do his normal work. He may be sluggish and stubborn if he's not feeling up to par. If this unusual behavior lasts more than a day or two, ask your veterinarian to see if he can find something wrong with him. A sore leg or tooth can make a horse irritable.

Too much feed and too little work: If a horse is given too much high-energy feed and doesn't do enough work, he will be frisky and full of himself—with tons of extra energy for bucking and bolting! If he is overly rambunctious, give him a low-energy feed (one without oats). You could also cut down on his concentrates and replace them with low-energy roughage such as hay.

If your horse is too full of beans, let him spend a lot of time out in a field or turn-out area to burn off excess energy. You can also lunge him until he settles down, but it's better to simply adjust his feed.

Rider problems: Bad riding makes a horse misbehave. Bouncing around on his back can make him sore and grumpy, and he may buck. Yanking on his mouth can hurt it, and he may rear to escape the pain. If you're having a lot of problems with your horse, you may need to evaluate your riding skills. Are you a good enough rider for him? If you feel that you're not clicking with your horse, sign up for lessons with a good instructor.

If you're having problems with your horse, sign up for lessons.

If you cannot solve a behavioral problem by yourself, seek help before the problem gets worse. (And it will!) If you take lessons, describe your horse's behavior to your instructor and see if she can devise a plan of action. She may want to spend time with your horse to see what he's doing. If she is an experienced horse person, she may come up with some solutions you haven't considered.

She may want to ride your horse for a few weeks to see if she can sort out the problem.

She may want to keep him at her facility too. Think twice before giving your horse to your instructor to be "sorted out." You shouldn't expect your horse to be perfect a certain number of weeks later. It's likely that the problem will return when you start riding him again. It's better to work with your instructor to solve the problem. You need to ride your horse too. If you're nervous about the problem, stick to riding only when your instructor is around.

FALLING OFF

Even Olympic-caliber riders fall off, because no one is immune to eating dirt occasionally! In fact, as you gain experience and take on more challenging activities such as jumping or riding cross-country, you are more likely to fall off.

If you think you're about to fall off your horse, you may have to take desperate measures to stay in the saddle. Lean down as close as you can to your horse's neck, and wrap your arms around him for security. This is no time to worry about your position!

If you can't stay in the saddle, here are two things to remember:

1. Let go of the reins! If you hang on to them, your horse could drag you along, and he may step on you. Your horse probably won't go too far without you, especially if there is some tasty grass around, so let go. It is better to have broken reins than a broken arm.

2. Curl up in a ball as you fall: This method is used successfully by jockeys, who fall off a lot! Don't hold your arms out to break the fall. The only thing you'll break is an arm. Keep your arms close to your sides and roll when you hit the ground.

Let go of the reins if you fall off!

If you fall off and think you have been injured, it's best to lie quietly for a moment or two, then get up slowly. With luck, other riders will come to your aid. If you have a serious fall, don't let anyone take off your helmet. Moving your head and neck could cause further injury. Lie still and wait until a rescue crew comes. Let a member from the crew remove your helmet and test you for broken bones. If you watch another rider take a tumble, leave his or her helmet on until help arrives.

BUCKING

When a horse bucks, he puts his head down, arches his back, and kicks his hind legs in the air. A horse may buck if his saddle is pinching him or if he is feeling grumpy. Others buck if they have too much energy and are a bit "high." Some horses, mostly naughty ones, buck to remove pesky riders!

If your horse puts his head down and you think he is going to buck, tug on his reins quickly to get his head up and kick him to get him moving forward. It is difficult for a horse to buck if he is moving.

Sit deep in the saddle and lean backward on a bucking horse. If you lean forward, you will end up on the ground. Don't hit your horse with a crop or punish him severely if he bucks. It's best to ignore bucking and keep him working hard. If you make a big deal out of bucking, he may do it more.

BOLTING

When a horse gallops off with you at top speed and you lose control of him, it's called bolting. A horse may bolt because he is scared or overly excited. He may not look where he's going and could knock people or other horses over. Bolting can be very scary, but it's essential that you stay calm so you can stop your horse as soon as possible. Experienced riders use a method called the pulley rein to stop a bolting horse. Here's how you do it:

Use the pulley rein to stop a bolting horse.

1. Sit deep in the saddle.

2. Shorten your reins as much as you can.

3. Put one hand on the horse's withers and pull back sharply with the other hand. Give the rein a good tug. Continue pulling with one rein until he turns his head toward you. If he doesn't turn, try the other rein.

4. Circle! Circle! Circle! It's hard for a horse to continue galloping when he is going round in a tight circle. Make the circle smaller and smaller until he slows down.

REARING

Rearing is when a horse stands up on his hind legs. This might be entertaining in an old western movie, but it's very dangerous. If your horse rears a lot, consider selling him. He's not safe.

A horse may rear because he doesn't want to move forward. He may also rear if he's upset or confused. Unfortunately, once he learns that rearing is a great way of getting out of work, it is almost impossible to get him to stop.

Never pull back on the reins if your horse rears. You'll unbalance him, and he could fall backward on top of you. If you feel that your horse is going to rear, turn him quickly or kick him so he moves forward. He can't rear if he is moving, so try your best to keep him working. If he rears, immediately loosen the reins, lean forward, and wrap your arms around his neck. When he lands, kick him so that he moves forward again.

Don't let your horse munch grass while you're riding!

GRABBING GRASS

Some horses think trail rides are one big salad bar. They put their heads down and munch on grass every chance they get. Don't get lazy and think to yourself, "A little nibble won't hurt. It's a nice treat." If you let your horse eat grass whenever he wants, he'll try to do it all the time. Grass grabbing gets annoying after a while, and you'll end up with a dirty bit, too. Keep your horse's head up and maintain firm contact on the reins. Your horse can graze on his own time!

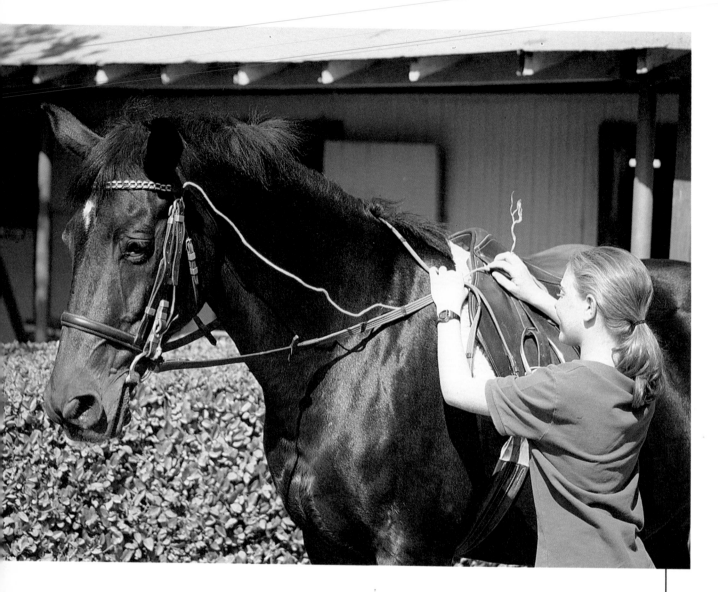

Grass reins keep your horse's head up and prevent him from snacking.

If your horse is really greedy or is being ridden by a child or an inexperienced rider, put grass reins on him. Grass reins are easy to make. Simply tie a long piece of twine to each bit ring. Then run the twine up alongside the cheekpiece and through the browband loop. Finally, tie the twine to the metal D-rings on both sides of the saddle. The twine should be short enough to stop your horse from lowering his head to graze, but long enough so he can bob his head freely as he moves.

KICKING

Be very careful around a horse who kicks. Try to stay away from his hindquarters and well out of his kicking range. If you must walk behind a kicker, and he is tied up, stay very close to him. It's hard for him to kick you if you are within a foot or two.

If you have a horse who kicks other horses, let everyone riding near you know about his problem so they can give him plenty of room.

If your horse lifts his leg or acts aggressively toward another horse, give him a hard whack behind your leg with a whip and say "No!" in a firm voice. Then ask him to move forward. If he is working hard, he shouldn't have time to think about kicking.

If you go to a show or on a trail ride with other horses and riders, tie a red ribbon on your horse's tail. This warns others that he kicks.

A red ribbon tied to a horse's tail warns others that he kicks.

Chapter Eight

Having Fun with Your Horse

As you become a more experienced rider, you'll realize there's more to riding than endlessly trotting around a ring. You will seek out new challenges and find a lot of fun activities you and your horse can do together. Getting out of the ring and going trail riding or to shows can be beneficial to both you and your horse. Varying your riding routine helps keep you motivated as a rider and offers you new goals to work toward. You'll meet new horse people and broaden your knowledge of riding. In addition, getting out and about prevents your horse from getting bored with life. When a horse is bored, she may behave badly and act grumpy. Let's look at some exciting activities that will keep you and your horse busy.

Trail riding is fun for both you and your horse.

TRAIL RIDING

There is nothing quite like riding in the open with your horse. Exploring woodsy trails or cantering across large fields is exhilarating, and your horse should enjoy it as much as you do. Trail riding is great exercise for your horse and gives her a much-needed break from schooling. You should try to get out of the ring as much as possible.

If you live in an urban area with no trails, find out if there are any state parks nearby that have riding trails. You may be able to trailer your horse to one of them for the day. Some parks have lovely, well-groomed trails and areas where you can put your horse in a corral while you have a picnic. Ask if there are other enthusiastic trail riders at your facility and arrange outings with them.

Before you head out, make sure that you have full control of your horse. Even the quietest horse can get excited out in the open, and some horses may buck or bolt. You must be able to slow down your horse and bring her to a halt. You must also be able to mount your horse from the ground if you want to get off to open a gate, have a picnic, or use a restroom. There won't be a mounting block handy on the trail.

Part of the fun of trail riding is admiring the scenery, but pay attention to what your horse is doing and what's going on around you. Your horse could trip and you could take a tumble. Watch out for trash or other "scary monsters" such as fallen trees or old cars that might spook your horse. If there is a strange-looking object in your path that you know is safe, keep a firm hold on the reins, squeeze with both of your legs, and tell your horse to walk forward. Don't allow her to run away from the object or veer off the path.

Even though you're having a nice, relaxing time chatting with your friends, it's essential that you maintain a good riding position. Don't get sloppy. Keep a light but constant feel on your horse's mouth, and stick your legs to her sides. Your position should be just the same as it is in the ring.

Here are some tips to remember when trail riding:

Always ride with another person. If you are alone and fall off, you could be in big trouble.

Tell someone back at the barn or at home where you're going.

Carry some change or a cellular phone with you, in case you have to make a phone call if you get in a jam.

Carry a hoof pick in a pocket. Rocks or mud in your horse's hooves could make her lame.

If you are going out for several hours, keep your horse's halter on underneath her bridle and fasten a tied-up lead rope to the D-ring on the saddle. You might want to stop and let your horse graze, or tie her up while you have a picnic or a rest.

Carry your driver's license or some other form of identification in a pocket.

Have a dog collar disc engraved with your name and phone number, and attach it to a D-ring on the saddle.

If you ride on other people's land, stick to the trail. Don't ride over crops or get near cattle or other livestock.

Always shut gates behind you.

Cantering in a group can excite your horse, and she may get out of control. Only canter or gallop if you can stop your horse quickly. Steer clear of low-lying branches and grassy fields that could be hiding gopher holes or barbed wire fencing.

If you are going to jump over an obstacle such as a log, check the other side before you leap. There could be a hole or something that could trip your horse.

Keep at least one horse length between you and the horse in front.

Let your trail riding buddies know when you want to change gaits.

Alternate riding in the lead. A horse should be happy leading or following.

Always walk back to the barn after a trail ride. If you always return at top speed, your horse will jog or prance when you try to make her walk.

*Your horse must be in tip-top shape
to compete in endurance events.*

LONG-DISTANCE RIDING

If you love trail riding and your horse has plenty of stamina, try organized trail rides or competitive endurance rides. Both wind through great countryside and involve scrambling up hills and splashing through streams. Your horse has to be in good shape, and so do you.

To compete in endurance riding, you must train for weeks or months. Endurance rides are usually 25, 50, or 100 miles long, and because they are timed, the speed and pace of your horse is important. You will have to canter or gallop in places. A veterinarian checks your horse at certain stopping points along the way, and if the vet thinks the horse is not fit to continue, she will pull her out of the race and you'll be disqualified.

If you plan to compete in endurance rides, round up a friend or two to act as your crew. They provide you and your horse with food and water at the stopping points and hose your horse off if she's hot. To become a member of the American Endurance Ride Conference, write to the address listed in the appendix.

If you don't want to travel quite so fast, try organized trail riding in which maintaining a steady pace and using good trail etiquette are most important. Organized trail rides tend to be social events and may last several days. You might get to camp out with your horse. Contact the North American Trail Ride Conference for more information. Its address is in the appendix.

If your horse loves to leap, speedy jumper classes may be for you.

SHOWING

Showing your horse is one way to see how productive your schooling at home has been. You might even come home with a ribbon or two! Horse shows take place year-round.

To find out about shows in your area, ask your instructor or look for show programs at your local tack shops. Check local horse magazines for show information too. If you don't have a horse trailer, perhaps you and several friends could arrange to hire a professional hauler. If you board your horse at a big facility, there may be shows on-site so you won't have to travel at all.

There are a lot of different show classes, and one should suit you and your horse. If you have a well-behaved, talented horse, you could try working hunter classes. Your horse's performance is judged on the flat and over fences. Or you could enter equitation classes where your riding skills and the way you look on a horse are what counts. If you have a speedy horse who flies over fences, you could try jumper classes. These are timed, and the person with the fastest clear round (finishing the course without knocking down any poles or having any refusals) wins.

If you like a slower pace, try pleasure classes in which the judge chooses the horse who looks to be the most pleasant to ride. Or you could enter go-as-you-please classes to show off your horse's best gait. Many breed societies hold their own shows. If you have a spectacular Appaloosa or quarter horse, you'll want to show her off to other breed enthusiasts!

Generally, you're required to wear formal riding clothes at a show. At English-style shows, you may have to wear a dark riding jacket with long sleeves and breeches and boots. You'll also need what is called a ratcatcher, a plain button-down shirt with detachable collar. A helmet is

also mandatory at all shows. Your horse must be groomed until she shines, and your tack should be in tip-top shape. At more formal shows, you may have to braid your horse's mane so she looks really tidy.

It's essential that your horse be well mannered at home before you take her to a show. If your horse misbehaves in the ring, the judge won't like it and you're bound to feel embarrassed. If you are not sure how your horse will react at a show, take her to one but don't enter any classes. Simply walk her around and let her get used to the hustle and bustle of the show ground.

If you like showing, you may want to join the American Horse Shows Association (AHSA). See the appendix for AHSA's address and telephone number.

Most competitions require traditional show attire.

If your horse is extremely obedient he may become a dressage star.

DRESSAGE

Dressage is simply training a riding horse to be obedient and move forward in a balanced manner. When you school your horse on the flat, you are actually doing dressage. When you trot in 20-meter circles or halt at a certain point, you are doing dressage, too. Dressage is important because it makes a horse strong, supple, and agile, and it improves her coordination.

Dressage is a popular sport with competitions that take place all over the United States. Competitors memorize riding tests and perform them in a ring marked with letters of the alphabet. During the test, you and your horse must perform particular movements that start and finish at a given letter. Most tests include circles, transitions, and changes of direction.

While you are riding the test, a judge gives you a mark for every move. He notes the way your horse moves and how obedient she is. He will give you low marks for such faults as making lumpy circles, cantering on the incorrect leading leg, or halting crookedly. He will also penalize you if your horse misbehaves or shows resistance to your commands. Most judges have a helper, called a scribe, who writes down his comments about your test, which you can look at later to learn what you did right or wrong.

There are several levels of dressage tests, one of which is sure to suit you. If you're new to riding, you could try the introductory tests, several of which require you only to walk and trot. At the highest levels, horses must be able to counter canter (cantering on the outside lead) and perform difficult moves such as the pirouette (cantering in a small circle while the horse's hind legs stay in the same place) and the piaffe (trotting while standing in the same spot).

High-level dressage competitions tend to be formal affairs. Horses are braided and immacu-lately turned out. Riders wear black jackets with tails, sparkling white breeches, and top hats; however, at lower level shows, you can wear a short blue or black show jacket, beige breeches, and a regular safety helmet. Braiding your horse's mane at lower level shows is not always required, but a judge may be impressed if you make the extra effort. Your horse will look neater and have a more professional appearance.

To find out more about dressage, you can contact the United States Dressage Federation. Its address is in the appendix.

If you like galloping cross-country and jumping, you'll love combined training events.

When jumping cross-country, it's a good idea to wear a protective vest.

COMBINED TRAINING (EVENTING)

If you like galloping cross-country and leaping over fences, combined training may be for you. At the top level of the sport, combined training involves three different riding disciplines: dressage, show jumping, and cross-country jumping. It is designed to test the discipline, courage, and stamina of both horse and rider—and it's a lot of fun, too!

The biggest combined training events take place over three days. The competitors ride a dressage test the first day, gallop over a cross-country course of natural-looking fences on the second day, and pop over a show jumping course the third. The competitors are assessed penalty points for any mistakes they make in the three phases, for instance, not completing a dressage move or refusing a fence. The competitor with the least penalties wins.

At the lower levels of the sport, combined training competitions often take place on one day and may not require all three disciplines. There are different levels of combined training to suit all sorts of riders and horses; for example, the fences at competitions range between 1 foot and 3 feet 9 inches.

If you decide to try combined training, you may have to buy additional gear. You need an approved safety helmet with a fixed chin strap, and some events require you to wear a special safety vest called a body protector.

If you'd like to know more about combined training, contact the United States Combined Training Association. Its address is in the appendix.

FUN AND GAMES

If you don't have a trailer to take your horse places, you can still have fun at your facility. Round up four friends and form a quadrille. This is a musical ride with four horses and riders. Pick some lively music, devise a dressage routine incorporating a lot of interesting movements, and show it off to other boarders.

Organize small shows for people who can't travel to outside events. Ask a local trainer if he or she would judge for a small fee, and think up some fun classes, such as musical chairs and an egg-and-spoon race. A costume class would be very popular for Halloween.

There may be some people at your facility who can't afford regular lessons. If several of them enjoy the same riding discipline, perhaps you could form a club and arrange for a local trainer or successful competitor to come to your barn and give a clinic once a month. Charge everyone a small amount to pay the clinician.

Not only do all the above activities improve your riding skills but they also make a welcome change from your daily routine and prevent both you and your horse from getting bored.

RIDING REWARDS

So, you've reached the last page. Hopefully this book has given you an understanding of the basics you'll need to master in order to develop a solid riding position and a secure seat. With the help of a knowledgeable instructor and a willing, patient horse, you should be well on your way to becoming an effective and sympathetic rider.

Of course, improving your riding skills won't always be easy. There will be schooling sessions when your horse completely ignores your aids. Lessons during which you feel frustrated and confused. Times when you fly through the air and end up on the ground. But all of these struggles *will* make you a better rider.

One day you'll be trotting your favorite horse around the ring, and she'll canter when you ask her—and she'll actually take off on the correct lead! She'll bend around your leg when you give her the subtle aids, and she'll jump a big fence perfectly. Before long, you'll be winning ribbons at local shows.

All of your hard work and time you've spent in the saddle improving your skills and learning how to communicate effectively with your horse will be rewarded eventually. And when you give your favorite horse a pat on her neck to praise her, give yourself a pat on the back, too. You have earned it.

Useful Addresses

AMERICAN ASSOCIATION OF EQUINE PRACTITIONERS
4075 Iron Works Pike
Lexington, KY 40511-8434
606-233-0147

AMERICAN CONNEMARA PONY SOCIETY
2630 Hunting Ridge Road
Winchester, VA 22603
540-662-5953

AMERICAN DRIVING SOCIETY
PO Box 160
Metamora, MI 48455-0160
810-664-8666

AMERICAN ENDURANCE RIDE CONFERENCE
701 High Street #203
Auburn, CA 95603-4727
916-823-2260

AMERICAN FARRIERS ASSOCIATION
4059 Iron Works Pike
Lexington, KY 40511-8434
606-233-7411

AMERICAN HANOVERIAN SOCIETY
4059 Iron Works Pike
Building C
Lexington, KY 40511
606-255-4141

AMERICAN HOLSTEINER HORSE ASSOCIATION
222 E. Main Street #1
Georgetown, KY 40324-1712
502-863-4239

AMERICAN HORSE COUNCIL
1700 K Street NW
Suite 300
Washington, DC 20006-3805
202-296-4031

AMERICAN HORSE PROTECTION ASSOCIATION
1000 29th Street #T-100
Washington, DC 20007-3820
202-965-0500

AMERICAN HORSE SHOWS ASSOCIATION
220 East 42nd Street
Suite 409
New York, NY 10017
212-972-2472

AMERICAN MORGAN HORSE ASSOCIATION
PO Box 960
Shelburne, VT 05482-0960
802-985-4944

AMERICAN MUSTANG AND BURRO ASSOCIATION
PO Box 788
Lincoln, CA 95648
916-633-9271

AMERICAN PAINT HORSE ASSOCIATION
PO Box 961023
Fort Worth, TX 76161-0023
817-439-3400

AMERICAN QUARTER HORSE ASSOCIATION
PO Box 200
Amarillo, TX 79168-0001
806-376-4811

AMERICAN RIDING INSTRUCTORS ASSOCIATION (ARIA)
PO Box 282
Alton Bay, NH 03810-0282
603-875-4000

AMERICAN SADDLEBRED HORSE ASSOCIATION
4093 Iron Works Pike
Lexington, KY 40511-8434
606-259-2742

AMERICAN TRAILS
1420 E. 6th Avenue
Helena, MT 59620
406-444-4585

AMERICAN TRAKEHNER ASSOCIATION
1520 West Church Street
Newark, OH 43055
614-344-1111

AMERICAN WARMBLOOD SOCIETY
6801 W. Romley Avenue
Phoenix, AZ 85043
602-936-6621

AMERICAN YOUTH HORSE COUNCIL
4193 Iron Works Pike
Lexington, KY 40511-2742
800-TRY-AYHC

APPALOOSA HORSE CLUB, INC.
PO Box 8403
Moscow, ID 83843-0903
208-882-5578

ARABIAN HORSE REGISTRY OF AMERICA
12000 Zuni Street
Westminster, CO 80234-2300
303-450-4748

THE BUREAU OF LIVESTOCK IDENTIFICATION
1220 N Street
Sacramento, CA 95814
916-654-0889

CHA—THE ASSOCIATION FOR HORSEMANSHIP SAFETY AND EDUCATION
5318 Old Bullard Road
Tyler, TX 75703
800-399-0138

INTERCOLLEGIATE HORSE SHOW ASSOCIATION
PO Box 741
Stonybrook, NY 11790-0741
516-751-2803

INTERNATIONAL ARABIAN HORSE ASSOCIATION
Half Arabian and Anglo-Arabian Registries
PO Box 33696
Denver, CO 80233-0696
303-450-4774

THE JOCKEY CLUB
821 Corporate Drive
Lexington, KY 40503-2794
800-444-8521

NATIONAL CUTTING HORSE ASSOCIATION
4704 Hwy 377 S.
Fort Worth, TX 76116-8805
817-244-6188

NATIONAL 4-H COUNCIL
7100 Connecticut Avenue
Chevy Chase, MD 20815-4999
301-961-2959

NATIONAL HUNTER AND JUMPER ASSOCIATION
PO Box 1015
Riverside, CT 06878-1015
203-869-1225

NATIONAL REINING HORSE ASSOCIATION
448 Main Street #204
Coshocton, OH 43812-1200
614-623-0055

NORTH AMERICAN RIDING FOR THE HANDICAPPED ASSOCIATION
PO Box 33150
Denver, CO 80233
303-452-1212

PALOMINO HORSE BREEDERS OF AMERICA
15253 East Skelly Drive
Tulsa, OK 74116-2637
918-438-1234

PERFORMANCE HORSE REGISTRY
PO Box 24710
Lexington, KY 40524-4710
606-224-2880

SWEDISH WARMBLOOD ASSOCIATION OF NORTH AMERICA
PO Box 1587
Coupeville, WA 98239-1587
206-678-3503

TENNESSEE WALKING HORSE BREEDERS' AND EXHIBITORS' ASSOCIATION
PO Box 286
Lewisburg, TN 37091-0286
615-359-1574

TRAIL RIDERS OF TODAY
PO Box 30033
Bethesda, MD 20824-0033
301-854-3467

UNITED STATES COMBINED TRAINING ASSOCIATION
PO Box 2247
Leesburg, VA 22075-2247
703-779-0440

UNITED STATES DRESSAGE FEDERATION
PO Box 6669
Lincoln, NE 68506-0669
402-434-8550

UNITED STATES EQUESTRIAN TEAM
Pottersville Road
Gladstone, NJ 07934
908-234-1251

UNITED STATES PONY CLUB
4071 Iron Works Pike
Lexington, KY 40511
606-254-7669

UNITED STATES TEAM PENNING ASSOCIATION
PO Box 161848
Fort Worth, TX 76161
800-848-3882

WESTERN STOCK SHOW ASSOCIATION
4655 Humboldt Street
Denver, CO 80216-2818
303-297-1166

Glossary

aids: the communication signals given from a rider to a horse

bolt: to run away

breeches: a pair of snug, stretchy English riding pants that cover the hips and thighs down to below the knee

buck: to spring into the air with the head down and back arched

canter: a three-beat gait that resembles a slow gallop

crop: a short riding whip with a looped lash

cross-country: a race that includes such events as timed hunter trials and chasing events, both of which are ridden at speed over natural fixed fences

cross-rail (fence): a fence used for jumping formed by two poles that cross each other, forming an X.

diagonal: a pair of a horse's legs at the trot such as the right foreleg and the left hind leg

dressage: a form of exhibition riding in which the horse receives nearly invisible cues from the rider and performs a series of difficult steps and gaits with lightness of step and perfect balance. Dressage also is a classical training method that teaches the horse to be responsive, attentive, willing, and relaxed for the purpose of becoming a better equine athlete.

D-ring: a D-shaped metal fitting through which various parts of the harness pass

endurance riding: a competition that involves riding over long distances and types of terrain in varying types of climactic conditions; participants are judged on time and the condition of their horses

eventing: combined training, including dressage, cross-country, and show jumping

flying lead change: when a horse smoothly changes lead during a canter or gallop without reducing speed

girth: a band that encircles a horse's belly to hold a saddle on the horse's back

hunter: a horse bred and trained to be ridden for the sport of hunting; a show hunter is a horse who is bred to be well mannered and elegant over fences in English classes

hunter class: a class in which horses are judged over fences resembling obstacles that might be found in a hunt field

jodhpurs: a style of riding pants that are close-fitting and cuffed at the ankle

lead: the action by the forefoot that takes the first step when entering a canter and while cantering and galloping; a horse on the correct lead is on the right lead when circling clockwise and on the left lead when circling counter-clockwise

line: two or more jumps (poles or fences) set one after the other

lunge: to train or exercise your horse with a lunge line, a whip, and your voice

lunge line: a rein made of cotton or nylon, about 25 feet long, that attaches to a horse's halter

pommel: the raised part of the front of a saddle

post: to rise and sit in rhythm with the horse's trot while riding

rear: to rise up on hind legs

release: to loosen one's grip on the reins and thrust one's hands forward when jumping. This action gives the horse freedom to move his head forward over the fence.

sitting trot: sitting, not rising, while trotting; in English riding events, the judge may ask riders to sit the trot

show jumping: the competitive riding of horses one at a time over a course of obstacles; horses and riders are judged on ability and speed

saddletree (tree): the frame of a saddle

snaffle: a mild bit for a bridle

spot-on: slang for perfect or correct

stride: distance measured from where one hoof left the ground and the same hoof hits the ground

tack (tackle): saddle, bridle, and other equipment used in riding and handling a horse

10- to 20-meter loop: circles that measure 10 or 20 meters in diameter; a term common in dressage

transition: a change of pace from one type of movement to another

trot: a natural two-beat gait in which the forefoot and diagonally opposite hind foot strike the ground simultaneously

trotting poles: a series of colored poles set approximately 3 feet apart on the ground, one after another, over which a horse trots

turn out: to put a horse to pasture

withers: the highest part of a horse's back, where the neck and the back join